RED SKY AT NIGHT

RED SKY
AT NIGHT

Country & Garden Lore

David Mortimer

AURA BOOKS

Published in 2003 by Advanced Marketing (UK) Ltd,
Bicester, Oxfordshire
© David Mortimer 2003
Rural photographs © Oxfordshire Photographic Archive
Botanical photographs © Derek St Romaine
Photographs on pages 115, 121, 122, 134, 141 © Ardea, London

ISBN 1 903938 29 5

Printed in Thailand by Imago

CONTENTS

FOREWORD

When archaeological digs yield the skeletons of our distant ancestors, a thousand years old and more, we find that their skull measurements are exactly the same as our own. Their brain capacity, in other words, was no less than ours. We make a mistake if we assume that they were less practical, less clever or less shrewd than we are. Their lives, though, were dedicated to survival, as those of their ancestors had been, and as those of their descendants would be until relatively recent times. Growing and rearing enough to sustain the family and the village throughout the year was a constant battle against the odds, and the intelligence of our ancestors had to be concentrated on the practical business of understanding the land, the animals and insects that shared it with them and, critically, the weather. Their food, their medicine and even their clothing depended upon it.

Each generation inherited the wisdom and lore of those that had gone before them. Well before the time of Christ, the Macedonians and the Egyptians learned things that survive today in our folklore, and have been tested by science and meteorology. The injunction, for instance, to sow seeds when the moon is waxing, which was known to ancient Egyptians, is explained by the fact that showers are statistically more numerous than when the moon is waning, and the chances of successful germination are therefore improved.

When, in their turn, the Romans conquered most of the mediterranean and much of Europe, they added the folklore of the Egyptians (and some of their plants) to their own, and took it with them wherever their armies marched, Britain included. Onions, garlic, parsley, borage and nettles are among the plants the Romans bequeathed to our rain-lashed island. As Christianity spread in the wake of the legions, supplanting or adapting pagan rites and practices as it went, monasteries and nunneries were established. It was in these isolated communities that much of the Roman and pagan inheritance was kept alive by the monks and nuns who had to feed and heal both themselves and others in need. So the kitchen and herbal (or physic) gardens of these communities became the seat of country wisdom and lore, adding to it all the time through keen observation and experimentation. It was the Venerable Bede, the eighth century Tyneside monk who was our earliest historian and an accomplished mathematician, who observed:

> *If the sky reddens at night it foretells a clear day;*
> *if in the morning, it means bad weather*
> which survives today as:
> *Red sky at night, shepherd's delight;*
> *red sky in the morning, shepherd's warning.*

In the 16th century both the population and the wealth of England exploded, opening the way for the splendid Elizabethan achievements in literature, science and music. This was also the time that the first publications recognisable as gardening books appeared. Nineteen such books are known to have been written, eight of them on horticulture and eleven on herbs and, coincidentally or not, all of them were pre-dated by Henry VIII's dissolution of the monasteries in the 1530's. This suggests that the massive increase in educational facilities and the rising levels of literacy that were being achieved fuelled a desire to capture the accumulated wisdom of the homeless monks before it was dispersed and forgotten. Whether or not this is fanciful thinking, one of the earliest books to appear, in 1557, was A Hundreth Good Pointes of Husbandrie by Thomas Tusser. One can almost envisage a lapping flood of unemployed monks jostling at the harassed author's door to enquire if perchance, Master Tusser, you've heard this one because, in a quantum leap sixteen years later, he published Five Hundreth Points of Good Husbandry. His work (which, incidentally, was still referred to in the early 20th century) was written in verse, presumably because a good jingle such as

In March and in April, from morning to night,
is sowing and setting good housewives delight

was likely to be memorable, if only for the awfulness of the versifying. Many of the so-called old wives tales are also in crude rhyming form, doubtless for the same reason, and not a few come from Tusser.

But throughout the ascendancy of the monasteries and the flowering of literacy, country lore persisted amongst the villagers in their daily struggle to survive. Whether in the hands of "wise women" (sometimes accused of witchcraft by those fearing superstition), who were often the repository for this collective belief, or in the hands and herbs of itinerant healers, much of this old wisdom has been found by modern science to have an explicable basis in fact. Not all, however, particularly that connected with love and marriage. It used to be said that if a girl placed a four-leaved clover in her right shoe, the next man she met would be her husband. Neither science nor observation seems likely to bear that out!

WEATHER YOU LIKE IT OR NOT

THE CYCLE OF THE YEAR AND THE EFFECT OF CLIMATE

If you're fifty or more, you can remember a time when fresh fruit and vegetables were something to be enjoyed only in season. Strawberries, to take an example, ripened towards the end of June, and one sometimes wonders whether Wimbledon fortnight is a celebration of tennis or of strawberries and cream. Nowadays, the anticipation of those few weeks when the local asparagus, new potatoes, raspberries and so on could be savoured has been dulled to the point of extinction by the availability in the supermarkets of food brought in from almost any country in the world at almost any time of the year. In that sense, there are no longer any seasons.

This makes it difficult almost to the point of impossibility to imagine the danger and difficulty of life for countless generations of our ancestors as, year after unremitting year, they struggled with no greater ambition than to find sufficient to fill their bellies. Everything they did and everything they ate had to be wrested from the natural world around them. The house they built, the fire they made, the clothes they wove, the implements they needed and the food and drink that kept them alive, all had to be provided from the land around them by their own labour. Of all these things food, for both people and their livestock, was obviously the most immediately critical, and everything depended on the weather.

The most spectacular example of the effects of bad weather occurred in the 14th century, a period known as the "little ice age". There were twenty-five years of famine in the hundred years after 1272 (and virtually non-stop rain in one three-year period). On top of this, huge numbers of cattle and sheep were killed by disease, murrain, in the decade from 1316 to 1325. Literally uncounted numbers of people died as a result.

It is hardly surprising then that folklore was, and continued to be, obsessed with the weather. In pagan times, festivals were held at critical moments of the year – for example, at midsummer, to propitiate the sun and persuade it to retain its power for longer. Some of these rites continue today under a religious or secular guise, but most have their origin in an attempt to persuade the weather to be co-operative. Sayings and beliefs about the weather are therefore to be found in abundance. Even today, from the depths of our sofa, how many of us anxiously await the TV weather forecast, even though all we're praying for is a fine day at the Test Match rather than the survival of our family?

July was the month of greatest anxiety to our ancestors. This was the hard month, when the food stored from the previous year's husbandry was finished, but the new crops and fruits were not yet ready to be harvested.

Don't miss a row or you'll lose one of the family

was a saying associated with seed-sowing time. It may sound superstitious but if, through carelessness, you seeded less of your land than you could have done, it might mean the difference between life and death come the following July. It seems absurd to us now that the month of school holidays and summer vacations on continental beaches could be the month in which you were on red starvation alert, but if the previous year's harvest had been a bad one, you could be in real danger. So, from the very beginning of the year, weather eyes observed the skies carefully to read the signs of what was in store for the day, the month or the season.

TO EVERYTHING THERE IS A SEASON,
AND A TIME TO EVERY PURPOSE UNDER HEAVEN.

THE BIBLE

JANUARY

In terms of weather sayings, the start of the year seems relatively relaxed. What mattered most was the state of the climate when it came to the two really important periods – sowing and harvesting – and whilst virtually all weather-lore displays a degree of pessimism, only later in the year does a note of panic or unutterable gloom creep in. In January and February, country folk were simply looking for indicators to tell them how the rest of the year might turn out.

A wet January, a wet Spring betrayed the belief that the weather pattern established in the opening weeks of the year would carry through to planting time. The growing season could be shortened if a bad spring delayed sowing. But nor did one want it too mild:

> *If the grass do grow in Janiveer,*
> *it grows the worse for it all year.*

Our ancestors probably didn't dare to be too importunate in requesting the right weather for fear of antagonising the God or gods that controlled it, but one longs to unearth some such saying as "Blue-skied, frost–filled Janiveer; that will bring us all best cheer!"

Plough Monday, the first Monday after 6th January, was traditionally the day on which work on the land was resumed. As usual, tireless Thomas Tusser had a rhyme for it:

Plough Monday, next after that Twelfth tide is past,
Bids out with the plough, the worst husband is last

(the "Twelfth tide" being the twelve days of Christmas). In practice this was rarely the signal for a frantic rush back to the land, and there were many local celebrations or festivals, eventually ritualised by the church into Plough Sunday, to allow some dressing-up or horseplay before the serious business began again.

A "husband," incidentally, was a farming person, and a "wife" a weaving person. The Anglo-Saxons were comfortable with equal rights for the sexes, and indeed the language had no gender distinctions. They distinguished sharply between areas of activity or responsibility – hence "husband" and "wife" – but the two could overlap as necessity dictated, so that it was not uncommon for the weaving person to be found working alongside the farming person at certain times. This continued to be so, at least in the country, even after the Normans had arrived in the 11th century and turned the clock backwards on gender equality.

St Vincent's Day, 22nd January, was the day you were supposed to begin pruning your vines. A laughable thought to the wretches of the miserable 14th century, no doubt, but a reminder that over the last two millennia our weather has revolved in cycles of roughly a thousand years. In Roman times, and again before the Norman Conquest, the climate was warm enough to grow vines. Today vineyards again flourish in England – well over three hundred of them.

FEBRUARY

All the months of the year curse a fair Februeer

it was said, echoing the January fear that good weather occurring too early spelt trouble for the later growing season. And in case it was your ill fortune to be surrounded by half-wits, you could hammer the message home more explicitly:

If February bring no rain
'tis neither good for grass or grain.

or

Much February snow a fine summer
doth show.

Equally pithy, and almost a prayer, was:

February fill dyke, be it black (i.e. rain) *or be it white* (i.e. snow).

Happily, Candlemas, 2nd February, was soon on the scene enabling you to be very precise in your forward forecast because:

If Candlemas Day be fair and bright,
winter will have another flight.
But if Candlemas Day be clouds and
   rain,
winter is gone and shall not come
   again.

Corroboration came in the shape of a similar rhyme, but with an even more forward-looking tag:

Sun in the house at Candlemas, half the winter to come and more.
If't be fair when the blackthorn flowers, in May come winds and long,
*   cold showers.*

Our forefathers were obviously prepared to put up with a lot in February, confident that they would be rewarded later in the year. They noted that:

As the day lengthens, so the cold strengthens

and also that

If the cat in February lies in the sun, it will creep to the grate in March.

That did not bode well.

St Valentine's Day, 14th February. Why should the day of an obscure saint be that associated with love and romance? In fact there were two Valentines, not one, both martyred in Rome in the 3rd century AD, and both in February. There is no record that either managed so much as a come-hither tilt of an eyebrow, although the proximity of martyrdom is an adequate excuse. There was, however, a widespread belief that in mid February birds choose their mates for the year and, however mistakenly, even Chaucer adds his authority for this. The Romans celebrated the fertility festival of Lupercalia in the middle of February, and it seems probable that the church, in its efforts to eradicate or sanitise pagan festivals, took advantage of the belief in the romantic aspirations of the birds, with all it implied of springtime and renewal, to link this with one or other of the unfortunate Valentines, both of whom had come to their sticky, but convenient, end in the middle of February.

MARCH

March was the month of unrelenting ploughing, digging and preparation for sowing, but ahead lay the reward of the Easter festival – a time of feasting.

So many misties in March, so many frosties in May

was one of the sayings of the month, still with a worried eye on what the growing season held in store. Ominously, another saying added a grim overtone to this anxiety, proclaiming that –

March'll search ye,
April try ye,
May'll tell, whether ye live or die.

But at least better times ought to lie ahead and, as we still say today,

March comes in like a lion and goes out like a lamb

offering at least a touch of optimism, although we've rather forgotten the obverse of the rhyme:

If it comes like a lamb, it'll go like a lion.

But Spring lay ahead. March is the month of the Spring equinox and 21st March is its official harbinger. On that day, the amount of light and darkness is equally balanced – exactly twelve hours of each. In the country, the cycle of cultivation is released because increasing light and increasing warmth come together. What more natural, therefore, than to find that the coming of the Spring equinox should be a time of rejoicing and celebration.

Eostre, the Goddess of Dawn, was the greatest of all pagan festivals, on which a human victim was annually sacrificed and buried in the belief that the growth and fruition of the crops was the victim's body returning to life. How easy, and how obvious, for the early church to appropriate Eostre and convert it to Easter, the sacred festival of life given and reborn.

The egg as the symbol of the renewal of life and growth was worldwide, known to have existed in China and predating the birth of Christ by many centuries. Again, it was easy for the early church to adopt the egg as an object of Easter veneration fitting, as it so neatly did, the belief in life given back. Following the long abstinence of Lent, an egg was a welcome gift for hungry people.

Easter also marked the first great excuse of the year for a feast and, with the threat of famine never far away, it was an excuse enthusiastically taken by as many as could afford to indulge it. What is it that makes bitter things sweet? asked an ancient riddle, to which the answer was Hunger. But as April arrived, chickens, ducks, geese and pigeons might be candidates for the menu and, if you lived near fresh water, you might have access to pike, eels, brown trout, burbot or lampreys.

APRIL

April brings the sweet spring showers — on and on for hours and hours! sang
Flanders and Swann in the 1960's, going a little over the top as usual.

> *April weather;*
> *rain and sunshine both together*

went the old rhyme more realistically, laying down very clearly what it was
that country folk wanted and expected. If, in fact, it was on the chilly side,
so much the better —

> *When April blows his horn*
> *'tis good for both hay and corn.*

Another saying confirmed this:

> *A cold April and a full barn*

meant one could anticipate excellent growing conditions and healthy
crops come August. A good crop of hay for the livestock and of corn for
people was the first object of most people's prayers.

Compared to us, our mediaeval ancestors had few flowers, and had anyone
suggested to them that their main purpose was to look pretty, they
wouldn't have known whether to laugh, cry or escort the lunatic politely
but firmly to bedlam. Flowers were of value only if they performed some
useful function, whether as medicine, as tokens of good fortune or in
warding off spirits and witches. But, as the first gardens were established
as places of exercise and relaxation, broadly speaking from Tudor times
onwards, flowers also began to attract attention for the visual pleasure

they could give. However hard one tries to clamp one's hand over Thomas Tusser's mouth he, inevitably, comes up with a jingle:

Sweet April showers do spring May flowers,

but a century later Robert Herrick expressed it more memorably and more beautifully:

First April she, with mellow showers,
opens the way for early flowers:
Then after her comes smiling May
In a more rich and sweet array.

Trees, on the other hand, were both noble and utilitarian. Apart from their many other uses, they helped with the weather-forecasting:

Oak before ash, we're in for a splash:
Ash before oak, we're in for a soak

it was said. In other words, you're bound to get wet whether the oak comes into leaf before the ash or vice-versa, but the extent of your discomfort would determine whether it was to be harmful or life-enhancing. As the indefatigable Tusser explained, clutching bystanders by the wrist,

By sowing in wet is little to get.

As, indeed, more explicit regional variations on the behaviour of oak and ash made even clearer:

If the oak be out before the ash
there'll only be a little splash;
If the ash be out before the oak
then there'll be a regular soak.

MAY

Now growth was under way, and it comes as no surprise to us that the beginning of the month was marked by many celebrations, the traces of which are still to be found in the May Day holiday, despite its appropriation by labour movements and politicians throughout the world.

Now the cattle could be turned out to graze in the fields. Their condition after the winter months was a matter of concern, because

From Christmas to May
weak cattle decay.

None of them would be fat, but if their coats were thick, they'd be all right

In Spring, hair is worth more than meat.

Nevertheless, country folk believed firmly that a chilly May would produce the weather they wanted in June and July.

A cold May and a windy
a full barn will find ye,

meaning that the crops would yield well and provisions for the winter would be assured.

Warm May barn full of hay,

on the other hand, meant the grass would roar ahead, hay cutting would have to take place too early and the crops were likely to do less well, with the result that

A hot May makes a fat churchyard

– another of those merry quips with which to scare the children.

Nevertheless May Day revels were a sign that summer, whether chilly or warm, had really arrived. Youths of both sexes would disappear into the woods, often not returning until morning (thus causing, then as now, many a parental sleepless night) with May garlands composed of hawthorn (or may). Here we go gathering nuts in may is almost certainly a corruption of "Here we go gathering knots of may." Perhaps because it flowered early, hawthorn had great significance, indicating the return of new life, and garlands of hawthorn were taken from door to door to wish people prosperity. The old warning *Ne'er cast a clout till may be out* was a reminder not to remove a layer of clothing ("clout") until the hawthorn was in flower.

The Maypole was another great symbol of returning fertility and, despite much puritanical chuntering during the English civil war, dancing around it survived well into the twentieth century. The maypole itself might be a permanent fixture (Charles II erected a monster pole in London's Strand when he returned to the throne after the civil war, and it stood for fifty years), but more often the trunk of a tree was cut specially for May Day. The custom was probably Roman in origin, the tree being seen as a channel of returning life. Choosing a May Queen and a May King carried similar symbolic meaning, though the King eventually dropped out, leaving the election of a Queen to foreshadow twentieth century beauty contests.

JUNE

If on the eighth of June it rain, that foretells a wet harvest ran one saying, as country folk prepared to get thoroughly depressed about the weather. The jingles that have come down to us for the first of the three main summer months show a rather contradictory tendency;

> *Mist in May and heat in June*
> *bring all things into tune,* but
> *June damp and warm does the farmer no harm*

hints at uncertainty, whilst

> *A dripping June keeps all in tune*

seems flatly to deny the first rhyme. Perhaps this is simply the triumph of hope over expectation or maybe it's a reflection on the cussedness of the British climate. Byron, after all, said that the English winter ends in July only to begin again in August.

On St Barnabas Day, 11th June, it was believed you could, weather permitting, mow your first grass. This didn't mean purring around the lawn with the electric mower, of course, but hard days spent scything the meadows for the first crop of hay. Grass is (mildly) interesting stuff even if, for us, custom has staled its infinite variety. Most plants grow at the tip, so if we cut the top of the plant off it needs time to recover, if at all. Grasses, on the other hand, grow from the bottom of the leaf, so the more we cut them, the harder they grow.

Midsummer Fires and St John's Eve (23rd June)

On 21st June, midsummer, daylight hours reach their greatest number. The custom of lighting bonfires as the sun reaches its annual zenith is an ancient pagan practice intended to invigorate the sun and prevent its powers from waning. One would have thought that a few years spent observing how little effect this annual bout of arson was having would have spread discouragement, but it was a tradition that existed throughout Europe and lingers on today in many variations, from straightforward bonfires to hoops of flaming straw rolled down hillsides. These customs were especially strong in areas of more challenging climate, such as the Pyrenees and northern Europe.

Cornwall was especially single-minded when it came to setting fire to things at midsummer. All the hills of Mount's Bay, for example, would be alive with fires, and local people would foretell the future by counting the number they could see from a given spot. In the Isle of Man, such fires were also thought to protect cattle from murrain and crops from disease if the smoke drifted over them.

The church was not, of course, going to stand by and tolerate such a pagan custom so, with some asperity, it explained to all and sundry that they'd muddled up their dates and had meant to light bonfires in celebration of St John's Eve, which came along a couple of days later on 23rd June. In times somewhat sterner than our own, most people agreed, in public at least, that this was just what they had meant all along.

JULY

July was "the hungry month" and, in keeping, a pall of gloom and fatalism settles over the weather lore. Starting with a pessimism that was to be maintained, they said that –

If the first of July be rainy weather,
it will rain for four weeks together.

If you were lucky enough to escape July 1st, worse lay ahead:

St Swithin's Day if thou dost rain,
for forty days it will remain.

Unfortunately for our long-suffering forebears, they had reason for their despondency because modern historians of meteorology have established that the weather of mid July does indeed establish a pattern that lasts until 24th August, St Bartholomew's Day, and as we shall see that saint was little more disposed than St Swithin to be kindly. To be fair to Swithin, he did leave the door ajar, since:

St Swithin's Day an it be fair,
for forty days 'twill rain no more.

In times gone by, there was good reason for such a high level of anxiety about the weather. Not only was it the hungry month in which the grain stores were probably exhausted, leaving folk to grind old and shrivelled peas and beans into bran to make some kind of bread, but the hay barns were likely to be empty as well. *Make hay while the sun shines* was an important injunction for, if the weather turned wet when the hay was being cut and stored, it might rot in the ricks and barns with all that that implied for the well-being, or lack of it, of the cattle during the winter.

One can well imagine how carefully weather signs were observed to determine what was in store for the day. *Rain before seven fine before eleven* is a rhyme that endures to this day and, whilst far from infallible, often turns out to hold true. *Mackerel sky, rain is nigh* was another that is still widely believed, a mackerel sky referring to small mottled clouds in a series of rows, a little like the pattern of a mackerel's scales.

Animal behaviour was also studied for the signs it could provide. *If you see more than one horse rolling on its back in the morning, there will be a fine sunny day*, or so it was said. Cows vigorously swishing their tails were thought to presage a thunderstorm, perhaps with reason since the rise in humidity which preceded such a storm brought out clouds of insects to irritate the animals' grubby rumps. And we continue to believe, even in today's mocking and sceptical age, that a herd of cows lying on the ground means rain. Maybe they're simply keeping their next meal dry.

The dog days, so-named because Sirius, the "dog star," was in the ascendancy, compounded the uncertainty of the hard month. Lasting from 3rd July to 11th August, they brought humid, enervating weather to sap the energy and must have been hard to bear at a time of shortage.

AUGUST

August was the month when the rural economy went into overdrive. There were fourteen hours of daylight as the month began, and every one was used to the full. The wheat was cut, threshed and ground into flour. August 1st was Lammas Day, from the anglo-saxon meaning "loaf mass," the day when the first loaf could be made, and it is one of the oldest English country festivals.

The weather continued to be important, and already people were looking forward to what it foretold for September, the other important harvesting month.

All the tears that St Swithin can cry,
St Bartlemy's mantle (August 24th) *wipes them dry*

said country people, their optimism putting out frail feelers now the hungry month was past.

If the 24th August be fair and clear
then hope for a prosperous autumn that year.

But, alas, *If it rains on St Bartholomew's Day it will rain for forty more they say* and modern meteorology has confirmed the probability of this.

Banishing gloomy thought, if only for a few days, bringing the harvest home successfully was a time for great rural rejoicing and enjoyment. Often, harvest time was an occasion for communal effort, everyone joining in to help this farmer or that, and being rewarded for their efforts in food and drink. When reaping was finished, the last load was brought in in a great cart decorated with flowers and branches of oak and ash, drawn by garlanded horses. The men rode on top of the load, singing and shouting:

Harvest home! Harvest home!
We've ploughed, we've sown
We've ripped, we've mown
Harvest home! Harvest home!
We want water and can't get none.

Girls with bowls of water followed the cart, sometimes throwing the water over the men. That evening, the farmer held a harvest supper, with roast beef or other meats, plum pudding and apple pies. Ale or cider flowed freely, and there was singing and dancing into the small hours.

The corn dolly was fashioned, in whatever shape was common to the district, from the last stook of corn and brought in with the final load. The spirit of fertility was supposed to reside in it, and it was kept in the farmer's barn until the following year's harvest.

Just as the early church had taken over pagan rituals a millennium before and converted them to Christian orthodoxy, in 1843 the vicar of Morwenstow in Cornwall thought up the idea of Harvest Festival, which rapidly spread through Victorian England and remains common today, even though modern agricultural technology has seen the demise of the harvest supper in the farmer's barn.

SEPTEMBER

By September, the month when the orchards would yield their fruits, country people were recovering their nerve about the weather. True, you could never be absolutely certain how much rain would fall –

September dries up wells or breaks down bridges –

depending, presumably, on how St Bartholomew's day had turned out at the end of the previous month. But if it was fair on September first, it was fair for the month, and on the whole people looked on September with a kindly eye:

September blows soft till the fruit's in the loft.

September was not only the month for picking and storing the apples, pears, plums, peaches, quinces, mulberries and grapes, but also the time for slaughtering old or sick livestock, hanging and smoking bacon and making sausages and pies. Autumn produced acorns and beech mast in quantity, so throughout September and October, the healthy pigs roamed wherever they were free to go, fattening themselves up oblivious to the butcher's knife awaiting them. Pork could be preserved by smoking, but the availability of other meat in the coming winter depended on it being salted and packed in barrels and that, in turn, made salt a crucial and invaluable commodity. Even so, salt could only delay decay, and by the end of the winter the cook was having to devise ever stronger sauces to disguise the rottenness of the meat on offer.

Root vegetables, such as potatoes (once Sir Walter Raleigh had been thoughtful enough to introduce them to us early in the 17th century), carrots and beetroot were often stored in an outdoor clamp. The vegetables would be given a couple of hours to dry, and then laid out on a straw base. Different vegetables would be partitioned off from each other with straw "walls" and, when they were all stacked up, the clamp would be covered in a layer of straw before earth was dug out from around the heap to seal the whole edifice. A pipe was inserted in the top to allow air inside to escape, and thus prevent rotting. The clamp was a good device for preserving the vegetables whilst at the same time avoiding frost damage.

September was also a month for making candles in readiness for the rapidly lengthening hours of darkness. Beeswax, if you could get it, made the best candles. Such candles could be sold for a good price – fetching even more than honey, in itself a prized commodity, and the only sweetener in the days before sugar began to be imported from the Caribbean in the 17th century. But for the great majority of people, candles had to be made from tallow, animal fat, which produced an unsteady and unreliable light.

Well-dressing was a ritual of no fixed date, but carried out in many parts of the country. Water being a basic necessity of life, springs and wells have been venerated in all cultures from as far back as records or evidence exists. In pre-Christian times it was assumed powerful spirits lived in them, but the early Church quickly condemned such beliefs and rededicated wells and springs to one of the saints or, most frequently, to the Blessed Virgin Mary, the bringer of new life. The wells were decorated with flowers and green branches and ritual processions made to them in order to bless this life-giving miracle.

31

OCTOBER

A good October and a good blast,
to blow the hog acorn and mast

went the rhyme, reinforcing the fact that the countryman was eyeing his pigs, as they gorged themselves on their particular autumn harvest, not as friendly animals to have around the place but as a walking supply of winter bacon. Whether the harvest had been good, bad or indifferent, the worst was over by October and people could relax a little. They tended to look on the weather with an unthreatened eye, and writers have reflected this attitude. *Autumn softly fell, a harvest home, a slow grand age, and rich with all increase* wrote Wilfred Owen, whilst to Jane Austen autumn was *That season of peculiar and inexhaustible influence on the mind of taste and tenderness.*

Nevertheless, much remained to be done in preparation for the winter as well as in essential maintenance work on the land.

In October dung your field,
and your land its youth shall yield.

Even today, we're only too happy to get our hands on a few bagfuls of manure if we live within driving distance of a place where horses are kept, but until about fifty years ago smallholders, allotment holders and farmers relied on animal muck to fertilize the soil. Going back not very much further, human dung could be added to the list, and very good it was for the soil. This is another of those things that seems unimaginable to us in the twentieth or twenty-first centuries, but the flushing loo is only about two hundred years old, and outside privies with removable buckets for the waste are within the living memory of many people. (A flushing loo was, in fact, invented in 1596, but it simply didn't catch on. Was it considered hopelessly avant-garde, or did people prefer to use the little closet that overhung an ash pit below, from where the effluent could be periodically removed and dug straight into the garden?) As you will be expecting, Thomas Tusser is hopping from one foot to the other in his anxiety to offer advice on the subject:

> *Foul privies are now to be cleansed and fide* (purified)
> *Let night be appointed such baggage to hide:*
> *Which buried in gardens in trenches alowe,*
> *shall make very many things better to growe.*

There is nothing left to add.

Hallowe'en

Long before Christianity, the end of October marked the time at which summer ended and winter began. Hallowe'en was the day the barriers between the living world and the world of the departed came down, so the dead must be honoured. Ritual fires were lit to purify both land and people in face of the powers of evil, at their strongest on this day when pagan spirits or, later, fairies and witches roamed the land. If the fires were also fun, which they were, so much the better, and when the Church came along to appropriate Hallowe'en and turn it into All Saints Eve, it was wise enough not to deny the fun and games associated with the date. Fires were lit on hilltops and in open spaces, and in some parts of the country bands of young people would compete in an attempt to invade and scatter the fires of other groups. In some districts it was customary to roll barrels of blazing tar through the streets, and traditional games, such as ducking for apples or money, were common across the land, albeit with regional variations.

NOVEMBER

As the end of the year approached, people were starting to hunker down for the winter, concentrating on essential work in and around the house. As in January and February, they observed the weather more for what it foretold of next year's likely conditions than for what it would bring the next day. It could be stormy – *November take flail, let no ships sail* – or it could bring early cold:

> *If there's ice in November that will bear a duck,*
> *there'll be nothing after but sludge and muck.*

A variation on the same theme indicated the belief that if cold weather came before the turn of the year it would be mild for the rest of the winter months:

> *If the ice will bear a man before Christmas,*
> *it will not bear a mouse afterwards.*

Following the English civil war, the puritans had suppressed many of the old festivals and, indeed, anything that displayed unseemly merriment, including the burning enthusiasm of the fire raisers of Hallowe'en. Although Charles II earned his nickname of The Merry Monarch by promptly reinstating many, or inventing new ones, he had not got round to the Hallowe'en bonfires before, rather thoughtlessly, he expired. Keen to revive the spark of the old festival, Guy Fawkes attempted to detonate Parliament and when, on his being caught in the act, 5th November was declared a public holiday on which bells should be rung and cannon fired, the general populace instantly revived the folk memory of Hallowe'en and, before you could say Gunpowder Plot, were holding torchlit parades, lighting bonfires and rolling burning tar barrels down the nearest hills with old-fashioned gusto.

DECEMBER

A good winter brings a good summer it was thought and, just as a hot May might be fatal, the December warning went: *A green Yule makes a fat kirk-yard*. Despite having only a fraction of our many devices for keeping cosy and snug in the milder, globally-warmed winters of the 21st century, our ancestors were prepared to welcome severe weather because, in their eyes, it promised good growth next year.

> *A foot deep of rain will kill hay and grain;*
> *but three feet of snow will make them grow mo'.*

Even now, partying was not quite over for the year. Wassailing dates back to early times. The anglo-saxon words "wass hael" mean to your good health, and whether it's slainte, skol, prost, santé or cheers we keep the custom alive every time we raise a glass in company. In times gone by, though, wassailing was a Christmas or New Year occasion, generally practised by poorer people who would take an empty bowl, decorate it and go from house to house, begging for drink to fill the bowl and singing a wassailing song in return. The last verse of one of the best-known songs ends –

> *Come butler, come bring us a bowl of the best,*
> *and we hope then in heaven your soul it shall rest.*
> *But if you shall bring us a bowl of the small –*
> *then down fall the butler, the beer, bowl and all.*

Apple trees were commonly on the end of some vigorous wassailing. Folk would gather round a tree in the orchard, sing songs, pour cider over the roots and drive away evil spirits by whipping the trunk with rods, banging pans, blowing horns or firing guns to ensure a good, disease-free crop the following year.

I'VE DUG A HOLE — WHAT MORE DO YOU WANT?

PLANTING AND GROWING

Since Thomas Tusser is evidently determined to make his mark on this book, we might as well let him off the leash straight away:

Good huswifes in sommer will save their own seedes
against the next yeere, as occasion needes.
One seede for another to make an exchange,
with fellowlie neighbourhood seemeth not strange.

The 19th century saw the appearance – at least on any sort of scale – of the seedsman, and the 20th century witnessed the growth of the nursery which, in turn, converted itself into the semi-industrial garden centre, but before that time you were dependent on your own garden and your own efforts to gather the seeds for next year from your current plantings as they matured. You might be able to buy or exchange seeds in the local market but, in all probability, many did just what excitable Mr Tusser advocated and bartered seeds with their neighbours.

NUTRIENTS – OR GOOD, PLAIN MUCK

Naturally enough, and as we've already seen, you need to dig plenty of nutrients into the soil – manure, in short – before you start sowing your seed.

The better the muck, the better the luck.

Your own compost is an excellent starting point and all organic matter, weeds included, can be tossed onto the compost heap so long as you turn it from time to time so that the layer on top becomes transferred into the middle. There the heat generated will kill off any weeds still harbouring malevolent thoughts of plaguing you with continued growth.

The snag with compost, as with leaf mould or bonfire ash, is that it doesn't suit the impatient temperament. As with almost everything to do with nature, you have to be content to fall in with the rhythm of the seasons – which means waiting at least a year. It's the compost at the bottom of the heap that will be the most desirable. After a year, it should be rotted down well enough to be used as a mulch (i.e. spread on the surface around the plants) or to be dug in, but if you can bear to hang on for another year, your compost should have reached the point at which it's almost indistinguishable from rich soil. Your plants will be clapping their leaves in appreciation as they see a barrow load of this root-smacking feast approaching.

Much the same can be said of bonfire ash – always assuming you are not surrounded by the self-righteous who write to the local rag in protest if they detect so much as a wisp of smoke curling above the garden fence. The ash must be free of any chemicals or household waste and, even then, needs to be stored in a dry place (or mixed into the compost heap) for a year before it is succulent enough to exude any sex appeal for your plants. This is also true of leaf mould, which is excellent for enriching dry, stony soil in particular. Fill black polythene bags with your fallen leaves in the autumn, by all means, and, having sealed the bags with an old brick, puncture them with a hole here and there to let the air in – then wait for nine months or a year for it to become a gooey, fertile mess! You may not like the look of it, but you're not a plant.

If you spend your life within hailing distance of the rear ends of animals, however, you can eliminate the waiting and get mucking straight away. Horse manure, well mixed with straw, is good for heavy ground containing clay, which it helps to break up. Cow dung acts less quickly than its equine equivalent, partly because the cow is much more efficient at extracting all the available nutrients from the grass it eats. Not for nothing, as it stands there looking ruminative, does it pass its food through seven stomachs, so that what eventually emerges from the other end contains rather less of value than the horse can contrive. Nevertheless, once dug into your soil, its effects last longer. Pig dung is excellent stuff for helping vegetables along although – a word of warning – you do need to mix it with earth or organic litter before using it.

If you keep chickens, let them run around under the fruit trees they used to say and, indeed, chicken manure is very helpful to fruit trees, plums especially, which may explain why the brainless birds were often kept in orchards. But chicken dung is surprisingly potent stuff, and it will damage more tender plants in the general garden if it's not mixed with dry soil before use.

Since I can't envisage a rush to the countryside on a moonlit night to shovel cow or pig manure into polythene sacks, and since most local garden centres now stock many kinds of excellent, chemical free (just read the label carefully) fertilisers, it's time to get on to the interesting bits – the sowing and planting. But one last word of advice as we do so – if you're buying a general fertiliser, as opposed to one specific to a certain type of plant, such as roses or tomatoes, check that it contains the three ingredients essential for good growth – nitrogen, phosphorus and potassium.

How Much to Sow

There are many country sayings about the sowing of seed, most of which are very similar, and all of which add up to the same thing –

> *Sow seed generously –*
> *one for the rook and one for the crow,*
> *one to die and one to grow.*

The majority of plants produce seeds, berries or nuts in vast quantities, and if they all germinated successfully we would be surrounded by thickets sufficiently impenetrable to deter even Sleeping Beauty's prince. Their strategy for overcoming long survival odds is achieved by sheer weight of numbers knowing that, in spite of the insects and mammals waiting, open-mouthed, for the ripening of the seed, and in spite of soil or weather conditions that might deter successful growth, a few of them will, metaphorically, make it through the enemy lines. Hence the wisdom of the old rhyme. If you achieve a survival rate of one in four, you will have done well and if, as is likely given modern aids, you do even better than this you will need to prick out the unwanted seedlings to avoid overcrowding.

When to Sow

Never sow seeds when the moon is waning sounds like one of those pieces of ancient country lore that must be pure superstition. If so, it has lasted for many thousand years. In the 1960's Gavin Maxwell wrote that on the Isle of Skye crops were still being planted and harvested by the phases of the moon. The power of growth was thought to be in the waxing moon, whereas when it was waning it lost its strength and, therefore, anything that must dry, such as hay, wood or corn, should be cut at that time.

The scientific gods of the twentieth century have found the ancient maxim, which is at least 3,000 years old, to be true. Lunar fluctuations affect earth's magnetic field and its atmosphere and, since even the tiniest living organisms contain water, it is not only the seas that move in tidal fashion in rhythm with the moon. This makes significant rainfall more likely after a new moon as it waxes towards fullness. If you sow your seeds accordingly, they will get the benefit of a good shower or two to assist their germination.

Who needs scientific corroboration, in any case, with our very own Thomas Tusser to egg us on?

Fine seeds then sowe, whilst Moone doth growe.

With such authority behind you, you are on safe ground – although Thomas went on to except peas from the general rule, but why he did so is a mystery, since they welcome a good long shower much as any other plant. Perhaps he didn't like them.

Who in January sows oats, gets gold and groats.
Who sows in May gets little that way.

The question of when to sow was important, and to leave it too late was, naturally, to risk missing the best part of the growing season. But to plant too early could also be ill-advised and depended on where in the country you lived. It remains the case today that, as our climate – and therefore soil – warms from the south-west, the best conditions for planting in the south are likely to be roughly two weeks ahead of those in the north.

41

At Candlemas Day (2nd February), went another reminder, *'tis time to sow beans in the clay*. This sounds like misplaced advice because, as we've already seen, if Candlemas was fine, it foretold the return of winter. But there were, and are, those who advocate planting broad beans in autumn to let them weather the winter and get a good start come Spring. To do that is one thing, but since another old saying warned:

Sow beans in the mud, they'll grow like wood

planting at Candlemas sounds like a piece of advice it might not be prudent to follow.

Underlining the danger of planting too early, it was also said:

Apples, pears, hawthorn, oak:
Set them at All-Hallows-Tide (31st October) and command them to
prosper; set them at Candlemas and entreat them to grow.

In the autumn the ground has retained much of its summer warmth, so to plant shrubs or trees then enables the roots to get established and make their first growth before the ground freezes and everything shuts down for the winter. Conversely, to plant at Candlemas is to put the shrub into cold ground – the worst start possible, which even earnest prayer would be hard pressed to overcome.

Talking of prayer, reminders to sow came in biblical guise as well.

By the time Genesis is finished, your garden should be planted.

Bible readings in church followed a traditional timetable. Genesis was started before Lent and finished, therefore, around the middle of March, a very reasonable time to apply yourself to sowing, at least in warmer parts of the land.

And while the mind was fixed on heavenly things, it was also worth reminding yourself to:

Sow beans or peas on David or Chad,
be the weather good or bad.

In other words, get your peas and beans planted on one or other of the feast days of these two saints, 1st or 2nd March.

A FEW WORDS ABOUT BEANS

Quite a number of sayings connected with beans have survived idiomatically in English – *full of beans, not worth a bean, having a bean feast* and so on. The broad bean is our traditional bean and, for many years, it was the staple diet of the poor. Human nature being what it is and ever has been, it followed that, as your lot improved and you persuaded yourself (if not your neighbours) that you were rising in the world, the last thing that would be seen passing your lips was a (broad) bean. To be *not worth a bean* implied extreme poverty therefore, whilst *to have a bean feast* indicated either that a time of plenty had arrived or, if you were on a higher social scale, that somebody else's apparent affluence was not that great in reality. To be *full of beans* was applied originally to horses for reasons that remain obscure, but it meant, just as it did when humans inherited it, to be full of energy.

To demonstrate that the British were not alone in their dependence on the humble bean, the French say *C'est la fin des haricots* to mean that something is the last straw – if even the haricots are exhausted, there's nothing left to live on.

Whereas both broad and french beans have extremely ancient pedigrees, the runner bean is a real johnnie-come-lately, arriving in Britain in the first half of the 17th century, and for a hundred years being regarded simply as a decorative flower to be trained over fences and arbours. It makes you wonder who was the first brave soul to take a bite out of the seed pod and rush indoors yelling Eureka!

Before leaving beans and peas, a helpful piece of advice when you're cutting back in the autumn is not to pull the peas and beans up by the root, but to cut the dead foliage off at ground level. As you will see if you look, the roots have little white globules all over them. These are not a fungus, or something to be kept from your maiden aunt, but storage pods for valuable nitrates. Leave them to over-winter in the ground, and they'll act as an excellent conditioner for your soil.

When to Plant Potatoes

Having seen the peas and beans safely into the ground, it's the turn of the potato.

When you hear the cuckoo shout
'tis time to plant your tatties out.

Excellent advice – but when, exactly, do you first hear the cuckoo? And do you have a cuckoo near you to beat out its steam-hammer reminder at the right moment? They are, after all, the housebreakers of the bird world, liable to descend on another bird's nest unannounced and set about flinging everything over the side. In fact, cuckoos tend to favour known areas and keep on returning to them in the manner of successful but over-confident burglars so, if you're accustomed to hearing them in the spring, the chances are you'll continue to do so. But it could be any time from mid March to early May, which is none too helpful where the spuds are concerned.

There is an equally well-established piece of lore which nominates Good Friday as the ideal day for planting but, like the cuckoo's call, this too can slither around elusively within a four or five week range. In practice, you're unlikely to go too far wrong if you take the second week of April as a benchmark, making a seven to ten day allowance for the part of the country you live in.

MORNING OR EVENING?

Whatever you do, though, don't go away thinking that country lore is content with vague reminders of the approximate date on which to sow. Cometh the day, cometh the hour! And if you thought that taking the moon into account was rule enough, you'd forgotten about the sun.

In the morning sow thy seed.

It was reckoned that corn, and other seed crops, were best planted in the morning, while the sun was still rising. If, on the other hand, you're planting root crops or shrubs, the rule is

Plant in the evening, not the morning.

Isn't it aggravating? The second injunction does have reason to underpin it. In layman's language, the late afternoon, or early evening, is the time when the sun is waning and, in the all-important first few hours, the roots can enjoy the warmth of the soil without the risk of tender young leaves being scorched. Put more scientifically, plants use sunlight to photo-synthesise, a process most efficiently carried on before the sun reaches its zenith. During the night, they expire carbon dioxide through the underside of the leaf and take in oxygen, converting sugar into energy and expanding their cells or, in plain language, growing.

TO BE CONSTANT, IN NATURE WERE INCONSTANCY

ABRAHAM COWLEY

It's harder to find convincing reason to sow seed in the morning, although it is true that seeds enjoy early warmth to kick-start their germination. In a small garden, it would be better to pour a little hot water into the seed bed immediately before sprinkling the seed into it; or to fill a watering can with lukewarm water and pour a little over the covered bed an hour or so after sowing. A farmer could hardly do this on an industrial scale, however, and perhaps the next best thing was to let the waxing sun provide as much early warmth as possible.

WHERE TO PLANT

If you want to grow vegetables but are worried by a shortage of space, you can grow them in small clumps among the flowers, taking heart from the knowledge that this is exactly how it has always been done in cottage gardens. Only the arrival of the industrial seed drill gave us the idea that everything should be planted in neat rows, and whilst this is all very well for the farmer with large acres to cultivate, there are several reasons why "untidy" clumps among the flowers make a lot of sense.

> ADAM WAS A GARDENER, AND GOD WHO MADE HIM SEE
> THAT HALF A PROPER GARDENER'S WORK IS DONE
> UPON HIS KNEES.
>
> *RUDYARD KIPLING*

First, they blend in with the surrounding flowers very well. Secondly, it's much easier to plant little and often, with the result that the vegetables will yield over a longer season, giving you the pleasure of really fresh-tasting produce on a scale you can manage, rather than finding yourself picking a mountain of lettuces, or a bucketful of runner beans, and having to tramp the streets trying to thrust half of them into the trembling hands of apprehensive neighbours. The third reason is the best of all because, by growing your vegetables amongst a variety of other plants, you get their protection. As we will see in a later chapter there are plants, like the marigold, that repel harmful insects. There are others that attract "good" insects which like nothing better than to put their bibs on and tuck into a meal of aphids or others whose popularity stakes around the garden are on a par with those of politicians or journalists.

CROP ROTATION

Yet another advantage of growing your vegetables as to the cottage born is that it makes it that much easier to follow the sound principles of crop rotation. *Never grow herbs in the same spot twice* they used to say, and the rule applies to more than just herbs. Different plants take different nutrients or phosphates from the soil so, despite your best efforts to rejuvenate your soil with manure and other fertilisers, you will help yourself to enjoy produce which is bursting with rude health if you vary the location in which you sow from year to year. Since grubs can over-winter in the soil, you'll also help to sow confusion in their minds and deprive them of the satisfaction of knowing where their next meal is coming from.

In the large kitchen gardens of great Victorian houses, there was generally a strict and carefully-planned order for rotating vegetables. Some plants like a generous helping of manure and some, like the cabbages, sprouts, etc, of the brassica family prefer lesser dosages. A given area of ground would therefore be well dug and manured and, in the first year, such crops as onions, potatoes, beans, peas and tomatoes would be grown there. In the second year, parsnips, turnips, carrots and beetroot would be

planted, and also potatoes again, since they like well rotted manure or compost. Finally, in the third year, the brassicas would use the ground before it was once more given large helpings of manure and the cycle repeated.

It was also said that you should *Always grow some herbs outside the herb garden*, which brings us back to the protection which different plants offer to each other. Some have developed defence mechanisms, whether through perfume or the secretion of natural chemicals, that repel certain kinds of insects. Lavender is a good example of a plant which has the happy knack of attracting bees whist being off-putting to many of the harmful insects, so plants grown within sniffing distance of lavender stand a good chance of benefiting from its protective aura.

GIVING YOUR SEEDS A HELPFUL START

They used to advocate sprinkling your seeds with the juice of houseleeks before planting them. This, they said, *would keep byrdes, antes and mice away*. They were on the right track. Houseleeks have some very helpful properties (which it was thought, in a rush of optimism, extended to protecting the house from lightning if grown on the roof!), but it is a bit of a labour to extract enough juice to serve the purpose. The modern equivalent is to dampen a cloth with paraffin and roll the seeds in it before planting. Well worth a try, and especially so with beans.

Old newspapers, cooking fat, hair and green bracken are all helpful in giving certain plants a good start in life. Beans, for example, like moisture at their roots even if they resent being sown in mud, so a layer or two of old newspaper in the bottom of the trench in which you plant them – along with some manure – will be much appreciated.

Rather surprisingly, hair – horse or human – is also appreciated by a number of plants, beans included, but on the face of it this is a bit of country wisdom that sounds suspect to us. Suspend your scepticism once again because, as scientists have confirmed, hair is rich in minerals and trace elements not easily found elsewhere. Perhaps, when next you visit the hairdresser, you should ask for a doggy bag to take the clippings home in.

Chopped bracken (when still green) is another good thing to pop in at the bottom of the hole for plants that like their root growth stimulated by a cool, moisture-retentive layer beneath them. Fuschias, in particular, like this and it is only the lime-lovers who should not have bracken thrust under them. In recent years concern about the effects of stripping peat beds and bogs has grown, and suitable alternatives have been sought. Chopped bracken is a good substitute and a number of responsible head gardeners, such as that at Hidcote Manor, have adopted it, apparently with good results.

Believe it or not, cooking fat (or a good old-fashioned lump of dripping, to hark back nostalgically to those prehistoric days about fifteen years ago when we were a little less weight and work-out conscious) is something beloved of roses and if, when planting a new one, you tuck a lump underneath it, it will repay you with some splendid blooms in summer. Roses are also addicted to banana skins, but this is something we can come to a little later on!

YOU SCRATCH MY BACK,
I'LL SCRATCH YOURS

ASSISTING HEALTHY GROWTH

Since our ancestors depended on successful propagation for their survival, it's hardly surprising that the sayings and advice that make up weather lore are rivalled in quantity only by those concerned with noting which plants make successful companions to others. The herbs and vegetables which grew in the garden next to the house were primarily the concern of the housewife, the husband being employed further afield for much of the time, and in this sense many of the sayings that came down to us can be christened "old wives tales". But as the gardens of the great houses began to employ armies of gardeners and under-gardeners in the 19th century, much of this lore was supplemented and added to by their acute observation and experience. It's also worth recalling that right up to World War II, schools in a great many villages taught the boys gardening (and carpentry) as a matter of course. An area of land near the school or within its grounds was set aside for regular gardening activity as part of the curriculum and, of course, much country lore was handed on in this way.

SOME PLANTS THAT HELP OTHERS THRIVE

An example of a common saying is:

> *Grow foxgloves nearby your store of potatoes, tomatoes and apples.*

It was widely held that this was a plant that helped to keep disease at bay and would deter the pests that were loitering with intent to devour the fruit of your labours. It was also believed, and there is some evidence to support the idea, that the foxglove gave protection to the plants around it, especially azaleas and rhododendrons, which explains why it was, and is, so often to be seen growing apparently at random in cottage gardens.

> *Let nettles grow amongst your currant bushes*

states another old belief, and again there is reason for it. Nettles take and store nutrients such as formic acid, iron, nitrogen, phosphate, protein and silica which, among other things, makes nettles steeped in rainwater for four or five weeks a wonderful fertiliser. They are also an insect repellent, so if you let nettles grow up amongst your currant bushes (or plant them in old nettle beds) you're achieving two things simultaneously – ensuring that the currants share the rich nutrients provided by nettles, and helping them resist disease. Indeed, what's true for currant bushes is true almost anywhere in the garden, but since you don't want to be yelling "ouch" and leaping backwards every few minutes, you're unlikely to want them growing too freely in the garden. It may be best, therefore, to confine the beneficence of nettles to that part where you have fruit trees and bushes.

Parsley grown among roses increases their scent.

It's also a protection and stimulant for carrots and tomatoes, turnips and asparagus as well as being useful and decorative in its own right. It was thought to be an antidote to poison, so our custom of using it to garnish the dishes we lay proudly – or hopefully – in front of our dinner guests is a signal that we're not trying to poison them and if, by chance, the cooking persuades them to the contrary, at least the means of survival are before them. It will, said a 16th century sage, *cast forth strong venome or poyson.*

Considering these good qualities, it's distinctly odd that parsley has attracted some very strange advice on the subject of how to plant it successfully. Not only was some of this advice connected with church festivals, but the secular warnings could be, to say the least, dire. *The man who grows parsley*, intoned one, *will have no sons and his daughters will be barren.* To make matters worse: *It takes an honest man to grow parsley,* suggesting that convicted felons were well out of it. It was further claimed that only the person who wore the trousers around the house would succeed in persuading parsley to grow. All of which suggests a bachelor with a clean driving licence living an abstemious, if lonely, life.

Why this extraordinary apprehension? Probably because parsley can be tricky to germinate. This gave rise to the saying that parsley seeds *go seven times to the devil and back.* That being so, it was recommended that Good Friday was the day to sow. It was also said that parsley should never be transplanted. Indeed, we've probably all suffered occasional disappointment when the young plant we've borne home from the garden centre goes yellow and refuses to flourish. The mystery could be explained by the fact that both seed and plant respond to sharp swings in temperature, so the remedy is to pour very hot water into the seedbed before sowing or planting.

Basil grown amongst tomatoes keeps whitefly away.

Basil has been around for a long time and, like parsley, is often used as a garnish. Once again, there's a good reason. It's a stimulant that settles the stomach and prevents nausea or vomiting. My 21st century advice would be never to use both parsley *and* basil together as garnishes if you're giving a dinner party – the messages you'd be giving out might drive your friends away for ever! But by all means eat a couple of leaves of basil before you set off for a party – it's an excellent way of keeping the tummy settled in the face of waves of alcohol. Four hundred years ago and more, people would take a present of a pot of basil as a token of friendship, and the Italians would do the same as a token of love, so it's obviously a herb with a high approval rating.

Growing it, on the other hand, could be tricky. Indeed, the advice used to be to wait until you were in a real old temper before you sowed the seeds, and then swear at them profusely as you did so. This was really a clue that basil needed hot, and even sultry, weather round about the end of May, and if you were hot too, so much the better. *Sow and swear, swear and sow*, they said.

I'm afraid Master Tusser is elbowing his way forward again, wanting us to know that best of all is to sow basil in pots rather than open ground and, since this is good advice, he can have a few words:

Fine bazell desireth it may be her lot,
to growe as the gilloflower, trim in a pot,
that ladies and gentils for whom she doth serve,
may helpe her as needeth, poor life to preserve.

Thomas obviously feels deeply on the subject.

Keep pests off raspberries and vines by planting garlic among them.

Garlic and chives among roses keep greenfly away.

The onion family in general gives off a pungent smell, in the descending order of garlic, onions and chives, and is a source of both repellent and stimulating properties. We know that onions and garlic also contain powerful anticoagulants to guard against blood clotting and cholesterol build-up, though science has not yet determined exactly what it is that makes their healing powers so effective. Inevitably, given their strong personalities, some plants, such as carrots and beetroot, thrive in their presence, whilst others would much prefer to be taking refuge at the other end of the garden, even if it means finding Dracula hiding amongst their leaves.

The list of sayings about helpful plants is long and even confusing, as an example or two may show:

Strawberries and cabbages are not best friends.

Plant strawberries near borage, beans and lettuces for their mutual benefit.

Peas and beans do well in the company of carrots, leeks and turnips.

Potatoes do well when planted close to peas and beans.

A small table of friends and enemies – or at least those not on root-entwining terms – may prove the most helpful way of sorting this out.

Name of plant	Friends with:	Disliked by:
Asparagus	Parsley Tomatoes	Onion family
Basil	Tomatoes	
Beans	Carrots Courgettes Leeks Parsley Peas Strawberries Turnips	Onion family
Beetroot	Onion family	
Brassicas (cabbage, sprouts, etc)	Thyme	Onion family Strawberries
Carrots	Beans Leeks Lettuce Onion family Peas Turnips	
Courgettes	Beans Peas	
Foxgloves	Azaleas Potatoes Rhododendrons Tomatoes	
Lavender	Roses, and almost everything else	
Leeks	Beans Carrots Peas Turnips	
Lettuce	Carrots Strawberries	

Name of plant	Friends with:	Disliked by:
Marigolds	Brassicas Peas Potatoes Roses Tomatoes	
Nettles	Currant bushes Fruit	
Onion family	Beetroot Carrots Roses	Asparagus Beans Brassicas Peas Strawberries
Parsley	Asparagus Beans Carrots Tomatoes Turnips	
Peas	Beans Courgettes Leeks Turnips	Onion family
Potatoes	Beans Peas Strawberries	Tomatoes
Strawberries	Beans Lettuce	Brassicas Onion family
Thyme	Brassicas	Potatoes
Tomatoes	Asparagus Parsley	Potatoes
Turnips	Beans Carrots Leeks Parsley	

MORE HELPFUL PLANTS TO HAVE AROUND

Apart from the herbs or flowers, such as Basil, mentioned in the preceding table, there are others which act in a generally helpful way to the plants around them:

Borage protects strawberries;

Chamomile is particularly good for cabbages and onions, and can be planted everywhere to give protection, since it improves the soil. If you need to buck up an ailing plant, put chamomile near it for a year or so, but remove it once it's done its healing work. After a while it seems to take over the other plant, which begins to fade again.

Dill goes well alongside brassicas, but definitely not with carrots.

Lavender, as we've seen, is thoroughly sociable and lives happily with anything.

Pot marigolds (calendula) keeps pests away from asparagus and tomatoes.

Marigolds (tagetes), like foxgloves, are still to be found dotted around in gardens as they have been for generation upon generation. Admittedly, they self-seed freely, but this is only a partial explanation for the prevalence of one of the friendliest little flowers around. The excretions from their roots, preceded by a warning aroma, frightens away a variety of insect pests, notably eelworm. For this reason, they are an ally to all sorts and conditions of plants which benefit from this security blanket thrown around them. That is why you will often see marigolds in the gardens of the cognoscenti, whether in knots amongst the flowers and vegetables, or at the front of borders. They are on sentry duty and, whether they are French, Mexican or African marigolds, you will benefit from throwing open your garden gate to them.

Not the least of their virtues is that the common Mexican marigold helps to control ground elder, one of the gardener's worst nightmares – or so, at least, many country folk will swear. Couch grass is another of the persistent weeds that may have you tossing, turning and groaning in your sleep, and for this a good sowing of turnips is said to be a capital cure.

A thick sowing of turnip seed will rid the land of couch, it was proclaimed. You may hate turnips, but not half as much, I dare say, as you hate couch grass. If you're afflicted by either of these monstrous evils, how much money do you spend on weed killers, or how many unavailing hours do you spend trying to dig them out? At least for one season, it might well be worth the far more modest expenditure on a packet of marigold seeds or turnip seeds to test whether the remedy works.

Rosemary provides protection against carrot fly and cabbage pests, and if sage is planted nearby the effect of its guard duty is redoubled, since sage repels cabbage white butterflies.

Thyme is another of those plants that is on good terms with just about all growing things, but is thoroughly disliked by cabbage root fly.

Even now the list of helpful plants is not exhausted. Continuing Nature's Neighbourhood Watch scheme, trailing or climbing nasturtiums are said to be helpful to fruit trees if trained around them, since woolly aphids and white fly dislike the scent, and insect invaders of the sort that shin up the trunks are put off, thereby encouraging the trees to fruit.

Another useful little tip is to cut a short length from a rhubarb stalk and push it into the ground alongside your cabbages (one per plant) if they suffer from club root. The oxalic acid in rhubarb is a preventative. (It's also claimed that a fresh carrot pushed into the soil by a cucumber plant will protect it, the cucumber, from wireworm – presumably because the wretched worm prefers the carrot (who wouldn't) and spends all its waking hours nibbling on that instead.

Nutritious Organic Matter

Quite apart from all the self-help that living plants offer one another, the remnants of dead ones, those that voracious humans have put to other uses, continue to be more than useful stimulants once we've had our wicked way with them. This is not very surprising since all organic matter, from bone to nail clippings or leather to hair, contains all kinds of minerals and nutrients itching to be recycled. As the church reminds us, *from dust ye came, to dust shall ye return!*

Banana skins are bursting with things in which many soils are deficient – calcium, magnesium, phosphates, silica, sodium and sulphur – and roses, especially, appreciate it if you dig the odd skin or two in around their roots just below the surface. When you've given each of your roses in turn a banana skin treat, don't forget to keep tossing the skins onto your compost heap.

Much the same can be said for *tea leaves* (or bags) once you've finished your afternoon cuppa. Azaleas, camellias and rhododendrons love a mulch of tea leaves, hot or cold. They really aren't fussy, though admittedly a mulch of tea bags doesn't *look* too good. But as far as the compost heap is concerned, it doesn't matter whether the tea comes loose or bagged.

Thanks to the yeast it contains, *beer* is a first class liquid food for flowers and vegetables alike. Hollyhocks and delphiniums particularly appreciate it in the flower garden, and most vegetables appreciate an occasional drop. The real drunkards, though, are the cabbage family who like their beer regular and often – once a week. It's asking a lot to share your pint with a brussel sprout, to be sure, but one must know one's priorities! If you really can't bear the thought of your plants getting the ale instead of you, even the dregs left clinging to the side of the can will help. Just rinse a little water round the empty can and pour it next to the cabbage, hollyhock or other object of your desire.

Much the same is true of empty *milk* containers. If you half fill the empty bottle with water and shake it around, you will be making a mild liquid manure for your house plants or plants growing near the wall of the house (the latter are always drier than those out in the open because of the way in which bricks and mortar absorb moisture from the surrounding ground).

Leather and bone have been mentioned, and they, too, are full of nutrients. Old shoes used to be recommended as food for peach trees, in particular, but are worthy additions to the soil at the bottom of the hole dug for almost any tree or large shrub you're thinking of planting.

Obviously only the leather should be so used – buckles, rubber or plastic attachments and any other synthetic materials should be removed or cut away first. Leather, tough though it is, is no more than the hide of cow or pig and therefore good organic matter. It is, incidentally, one of those quirky little facts that vellum or parchment on which, even today, all acts of parliament are written down before being stored as the official record of what our legislators get up to in their Westminster club, is made from the skins of sheep. The reason is that it is extremely hard-wearing. The oldest piece of surviving parchment is not far short of two thousand five hundred years old, and our own parliamentary acts go back practically a thousand years – still in good, legible condition. It's rather comforting to think that the Deeds of New Labour are all solemnly recorded on the skins of sheep.

Bones are another rich source of minerals, best used in a dry soil rather than a heavy wet or clay one, and are much loved by fruit trees and bushes and vegetables. This is a mixed blessing if you have a dog in residence – on the one hand you are more likely to have a supply of bones to hand but, on the other, the dog sees no reason for you to bury the bone. That's his job and, with his exceptionally powerful sense of smell, roughly forty-four times better than yours, he'll quickly find out where you've hidden it and dig it up. You can, of course, buy bone meal instead but, if you leave it on the surface of the ground, the dog will be delighted and you will see him going from one to other of the patches you've just treated happily licking the grains off the soil or the lawn. I mention lawn because bone meal is helpful in controlling moss. If you rake out the moss and sprinkle bone meal on the raked areas, it will help – but only help – the grass to reclaim the area and keep the moss out.

Seaweed is rich in nitrogens and an excellent mulch or plant food which can be bought in packaged form from garden centres. But if you live near the coast and collect it yourself, be sure to wash it very thoroughly before use to rid it of all traces of salt — unless you want to see the leaves of your best-loved plants turn a delicate shade of black. Many people living within fifteen miles or so of the south-east coast of England during the 1987 hurricane woke the following morning to find their gardens black. The winds that had raged across the channel that night carried the salt spray off the waves inland and shed them over a wide area.

THIS WILL CURE
ANYTHING – TRUST ME!
THE BELIEFS SURROUNDING
TREES AND PLANTS

TREES

A tree is a nobler object than a prince in his coronation robes wrote Alexander Pope in the eighteenth century. Trees once covered the land very much more thickly then they do today. Where now there are scattered copses there were once thick swathes of forest – dark, mysterious and containing who knew what kinds of spirits. Individual trees were majestic things, outliving man by hundreds of years, and the symbol of life infallibly returning each Spring. It is not surprising that so many ancient rituals were connected with the life-giving properties of trees, nor that so many myths involved people being turned into trees or vice-versa. Touching wood as a means of getting good luck probably arose from a belief in the life-enhancing properties of the tree, and it may have been translated by christianity into the metaphorical touching of the Cross to denote protection being given by the tree of sacrifice.

Even as pagan superstitions were shed (and the word "pagan," from pagus, means no more than a country-dweller), the tree continued to be a source of wood for fuel, for making tools and for building; it also featured, as we have seen, in weather lore; its leaves could help you gauge the planting season; certain trees protected against witchcraft, and so on.

OAKS

Of all British trees, the oak was, and still is, regarded as the noblest. It is often said that an oak tree takes five hundred years to reach maturity, is at its peak for another five hundred, and takes five hundred years to decline. There are oak trees reckoned to have lived for two thousand years. To pick up an acorn from the ground in November, probably already sprouting a small root, and to bury it in a shallow hole an inch deep, is a humbling experience. If its shoot is not browsed by a deer or a cow the following year, you have just planted something that may well be there, strong and majestic, a millennium from now.

You will also have done something jays are doing all the time – planting acorns. If you watch jays living near a wood containing oaks, you will probably see them flying regular missions, three or four every minute, carrying acorns out to an open field and pushing them into the soil with their beaks. As with squirrels, there is an instinct to bury a source of food before the winter begins and both creatures have an astonishing ability to memorise where they have buried it weeks, if not months, later. Research now in progress suggests that periodically during the winter, squirrels will revisit their caches, dig them up and rebury them, possibly to refresh their memory of where the food is. Luckily, enough acorns outlast the squirrels' and jays' appetites to grow into oaks.

OF ALL THE TREES THAT GROW SO FAIR
OLD ENGLAND TO ADORN
GREATER ARE NONE BENEATH THE SUN
THAN OAK AND ASH AND THORN

RUDYARD KIPLING

Of all our trees, the oak supports the greatest diversity of life. Whereas, at the bottom of the scale, a conifer is reckoned to provide sustenance for ten other forms of life, an oak tree supports over three hundred, whether they are birds, mammals, insects or other plants and funguses. And if in the autumn you wander through a wood containing many oaks, you will probably notice that, whereas the ones in the middle of the wood throw their branches upwards, seeking the light, and produce few acorns, the ones on the edge of the wood spread their branches wide and produce many thousands of acorns. In some parts of the country, indeed, the oak is referred to as a weed because it is so prolific. It is little wonder therefore that, if the fields next to woods were left uncultivated, they would revert to forest within fifty years – especially when you add the seeds of hawthorn and wild rose which birds excrete, having taken the berry or hip for the fleshy coverings coating the indigestible seed.

The oak was regarded as a sacred tree. In ancient Rome, heroes were awarded a crown of oak leaves as a signal of bravery; similarly, in modern America, the oak leaf is depicted on awards given for bravery. On pre-decimal British coins, oak leaves figured on the sixpenny and one shilling coins, but were subsequently replaced with the lion as a symbol of strength and achievement.

Perhaps rather strangely, in view of its otherwise good reputation, the oak was thought to attract lightning strikes – obviously a great hazard in the days when nearly everything was built in wood. Maybe this was because the oak tree was supposed to be the tree of the Roman god Jupiter and, later, the Norse god Thor, who were the bringers of thunder and lightning. Whatever the reason, it was thought to be courting disaster to use oak for roof timbers. To build a house near an oak tree was fine, because the lightning would hit the oak rather than your house – as long as you were not so close, of course, that the falling tree might have your number on it.

Even today, you can see many iron wall braces shaped in the letters S or X. Supposedly, S represents the thunderbolt of Jupiter, and X the hammer of Thor, and by shaping the braces into these symbols you invoked protection from these powerful dispensers of catastrophe – the very opposite of the reasoning behind the use of oak!

ASH

The ash produced puzzlingly different reactions in country lore. Like the oak and the yew, it was regarded as a sacred tree – one that should not be harmed. On the one hand it was regarded as a symbol of rebirth, the tree of motherhood and one which offered protection against witchcraft. On the other, it was regarded by some as the very opposite, the haunt of witches.

It is recommended not to grow an ash tree in your garden on the grounds that it takes large quantities of nutrients from the soil, making the ground around it unlikely to offer sustenance to much else. There are also persistent tales of peas and sweet-peas refusing to cling to stakes cut from ash, and of climbing roses trained to grow through the branches of an ash dying back to the point where they first touched the tree.

However, wood from the ash makes excellent firewood, whether newly cut or not, as an old rhyme confirmed:

Ash new or ash old
is fit for a queen with a crown of gold.

The wood of ash was also the recommended material from which to make milking pails, and since milk was important for the making of butter and cheese, this is no mean attribute.

Ash leaves were also lucky fortune-tellers –

Even ash-leaf in my glove,
the first I meet shall be my love.

And even more optimistically,

Even ash-leaf in my bosom,
the first I meet shall be my husband.

An "even" ash meant a sprig with all its leaves evenly arranged. This was not easy to come by – no more so than finding a four-leafed clover.

ELM

Despite the savagery with which disease eradicated most of the population not so many years ago, elm is one of our oldest native trees and it is therefore a surprise that so little folk lore seems to cling to its branches.

The appearance of leaves on the elm in spring was, however, a useful indicator of when to sow various crops., for example:

When the elm leaf is big as the mouse's ear,
Then to sow barley never fear.

Similar rhymes attached to planting kidney beans:

When elm leaves are as big as a shilling
plant kidney beans if to plant 'em you're willing.

Or

When elm leaves are as big as a penny
plant kidney beans if you mean to have any.

HAWTHORN

As with the ash, there is ambivalence about the qualities of may, or hawthorn. As we saw when talking about weather lore in the month of May, hawthorn knots or sprays were gathered and taken from house to house on May morning as a symbol of good luck and prosperity. But they were hung on the outside of the door or over the windows and not taken inside, for to do so was a precursor of death.

Hawthorn bloom and elder flowers
fill the house with evil powers.

This may be a distant hangover from the ancient Greek and Roman beliefs that May was an unlucky month. Although we commonly accept that the saying *Ne'er cast a clout till may be out* refers to the blossoming of hawthorn, it is just possible that, after all, it refers to the ending of the month, the unlucky month. The Romans certainly believed that May was not a good month in which to get married, and this belief persisted in Britain for many generations:

Marry in May, rue for aye

And if you insisted on knowing the reason:

Marry in May
you'll rue the day
and wed poverty.

This may explain why June is so sought after as a wedding month. Mind you, another old country rhyme gives advice on the right day, and it's far from reassuring to modern taste:

Monday for wealth
Tuesday for health
Wednesday best of all.
Thursday for losses
Friday for crosses
Saturday – no luck at all.

Does that explain today's high divorce rate?

Yet despite the dangers of the month from which it took its name, hawthorn was generally connected with wells and springs, and was the principal tree whose branches adorned them. When the Church took over these Holy Wells, it dedicated the hawthorn to the Virgin Mary.

ROWAN (MOUNTAIN ASH)

A rowan tree growing in the garden, preferably close to the door, was considered the best of luck (and to cut one down an act of indescribable stupidity) because it was the most protective of all trees against evil spirits, whether fairies or witches. Rowan branches were fixed over doorways and in cattle stalls, little crosses of rowan twigs were fastened to the cows' tails, and you were encouraged to use a goad of rowan:

Woe to the lad without a rowan-tree gad.

Churches would grow rowans in their churchyards as an insurance against the dead returning as ghosts. There are parts of Scotland where, even today, the belief in the power of the rowan to deflect evil is sincerely and firmly held. It is a tree whose wood is thought to offer protection against lightning and was therefore recommended as one to be used in the building of a house – as was the case with hazel also. Together, these two woods were said to protect sailors from shipwreck – a belief that has viking origins – and sprigs of hazel or rowan used to be worn by mariners in their hats.

ELDER

Elder brings the devil down the chimney it was said, and therefore it is very bad luck to use elder on the fire. This was probably because, if you do, it's prone to spit and throw out sparks with all the risks of a starting a blaze. On the other hand, elder was supposed to be (yet another) protection against lightning. Elder was also thought to be a hiding place for snakes, which is why, together with hawthorn, people were enjoined not to bring its flowers into the house.

APPLE

The apple is an ancient and abundant fruit, and one to which much folk wisdom attaches. The Romans knew at least twenty varieties of apple, and brought some of them to Britain when they invaded. Since then, the number of varieties has grown in number to two thousand or more, although in this country, what with EU regulations and industrial farming methods, the numbers are now in full retreat. When the 19th century Clifford sisters painted their series of watercolours, subsequently published as *The Frampton Flora*, they depicted twelve local Gloucestershire apples, yet today only three of these can still be found.

To eat an apple going to bed
will make the doctor beg his bread

it used to be said and – with very good reason – we still render this as:

An apple a day keeps the doctor away

because apple remedies abound in country beliefs. It is a mild laxative and, more usefully, the juice of the apple is said to heal cuts as well as promote good general health. Modern research has established that apples contain pectin, and pectin has germicidal properties.

The success of the apple crop was important, therefore, for more than just the store of autumn food it represented. The turn of the year brought the wassailing of the trees in the orchards and gardens – beating the trees and creating a din to drive away evil spirits, as we saw in December's weather lore.

Old apple tree we wassail thee,
and hoping thou wilt bear
hatfuls, capfuls, three bushel bagfuls
and a little heap under the stairs.

Then followed the anxious wait during the winter months until it was time for the trees to come into blossom:

If the blossom comes in March,
for apples you may search.
If the blossom comes in April,
you may gather a bag full.
If the blossom comes in May,
you may gather apples every day.

So far, so good – but isn't there always a big "but" where supposedly good things are concerned. In the country, it was said, no-one would eat an apple until St Swithin's day (15th July) was past. A light shower on that day was supposed to christen the fruit and to touch it with the saint's approval. All well and good, no doubt, but wasn't it also said that if it rained on St Swithin's it would rain for forty days? And if it rained for forty days was that not going to spoil the fruit? It makes you want to spit, doesn't it! Not even Tom Tusser seems to have thought of a jingle to deal with that illogicality.

MULBERRY

The mulberry tree was important in the local economy because of the silk worms it hosted, and mulberries are also delicious to eat. But the tree played a useful role – for which it was sometimes dubbed "the wise tree" – in foretelling the coming of frosts. The mulberry is very sensitive to weather, and does not begin to put out its new leaves until well after other trees have begun the business. Even the mildest autumn frost will make it start shedding its leaves, which makes it a valuable early warning system giving you time to protect other plants that are prone to frost damage.

HERBS AND OTHER PLANTS

For thousands of years homo sapiens has been pulling, poking, smelling and tasting the plants around him and working out the attractions or dangers of each. The Romans were writing about the properties of plants over two thousand years ago but, in the so-called Dark Ages that followed the decay of their empire, the semi-scientific knowledge they had accumulated became confused or distorted, first by a fog of pagan superstitions and then, despite the wonderful work of the herbalists in the monasteries and nunneries, by the attempts of early christianity to adapt these superstitions into other forms of ritual.

As the renaissance flowered in the post-mediaeval growth of economic prosperity, it encouraged an upsurge in learning and education, and produced a generation of enquiring 16th and 17th century minds to explore the properties of the plant world in their kitchens, and in the fields around them. Their published works were often called *Herballs*, and the most notable authors were almost always named John – John Gerard, John Parkinson, John Tredescant and John Evelyn. There was also Nicholas Culpeper who, probably because he wasn't christened John, proved to be somewhat unreliable. In a short and, one hopes, merry life (he died at the age of 38) he seems to have relied on a fertile imagination for much of what he wrote! On the subject of Angelica, for example, he announced to an open-mouthed world that it was

> *efficacious in the treatment of poison, pestilence, epidemical diseases, cholick, wind, pleurisy, cough, lungs, breast, strangury, shortness of breath, after-birth, stoppings of the liver and spleen, indigestion, surfeits, toothach and the bitings of mad dogs.*

Perhaps it was fortunate for the medical profession that in this, as in many other instances, Culpeper's enthusiasm out-ran his observation of fact, for otherwise we would need do no more than grow fields of angelica where doctors' surgeries now stand. Fortunately, his contemporaries and those who came after him were somewhat more disciplined in their deductions and writings, though this doesn't conceal some delightful turns of phrase or doggerel, such as Sir John Harrington's advice on fennel in *The Englishman's doctor*, published in 1608:

In fennel-seed this vertue you shall find,
forth of your lower parts to drive the wind.

As the French gardener and author Alphonse Kerr drily observed in the 20th century "At the end of three or four hundred years, it began to be seen that they had never cured anyone," – but not for want of trying nor of good intentions.

Nevertheless, a number of the benefits (and, occasionally, dangers) attached in country lore to some of the herbs and plants that follow have, in the end, been found to be accurate. In some cases, science has been able to explain why, in others we still cannot be sure. This, by itself, is warning enough not to treat this as a do-it-yourself medical manual. Deadly nightshade (*atropa belladonna*), for example, is lethal, and yet it can be found, in minute dosages, in a number of modern medicines. The secret is in the quantity used, the mix or the dilution. Definitely not a subject for amateur speculation!

Artichokes (globe — cynara scolymus, jerusalem — helianthus tuberosus)

Globe artichokes used to be thought of as aphrodisiacs on a grand scale. Culpeper was certainly not to be restrained on the matter: *It is no marvel that they provoke lust* he pronounced with relish. In this case, his fellow herbalists agreed with him, but these days we know that the globe artichoke is merely a giant thistle with tasty leaves!

The Jerusalem artichoke, on the other hand, is a relation of the sunflower and, for myself, I'm inclined to agree with Gerard that *they are more fit for swine than men.* Others may like them better.

Aubergine (solanum melongena)

The old English name was "mad apple" or "raging apple," probably because the immature fruit contains a poison called solanine, which doesn't do us an awful lot of good. The aubergine is, in fact, a member of the deadly nightshade family (but then so is the potato), but at this point the bad news stops, because in maturity the poison fades and it becomes good to eat.

Auricula

Also known as the mountain cowslip, the auricula was introduced to Britain in the 16th century. In those days, when a plant's life consisted of being pulled and prodded to see whether you could eat it and, if not, whether it cured anything, however imaginary, it was widely used as a remedy for headaches. Henry VIII and his Tudor offspring had a rather more abrupt cure.

Basil (ocimum basilicum)

Parkinson, one of the more reliable old herbalists, said that Basil *procures a cheerefull and merry heart*, and he's pretty close to the mark. We've already endured Thomas Tusser's commands on the subject of planting basil, so one need only add that, quite apart from its usefulness as a herb to settle the stomach, this pleasantly aromatic herb is excellent in some soups, in sausages, in pesto sauce, in tomato and egg dishes, and as a garnish. It also crops up in pot pourri quite often.

Bay (sweet — laurus nobilis)

Bay has been considered a powerful antiseptic for hundreds of years, and was used to relieve rheumatism, bruising, migraine and drunkenness or, as Gerard said, *to stirre up a decaid appetite*. Not a lot has changed. An infusion of bay leaves in a bath brings a lot of comfort to an aching body, if not necessarily to drunkenness and, of course, we continue to use bay leaves to flavour all manner of dishes, especially soups, stews and casseroles. If you want to freshen the air in a room, try putting a mixture of pine needles and bay leaves in a bowl.

One word of warning, however, should you want to grow it. It's not a very hardy plant, so you will need to have it in a large pot which can be brought inside during winter.

Bergamot (bee balm – monarda didyma)

The original form of balm came from the mediterranean, and has always been associated with bees, perhaps because its leaves secrete a kind of honey. Both Roman and Tudor writers recommended rubbing the beehives with balm so that *when they are straied away, they (the bees) do find their way home by it*. Bergamot, which has many of the same properties, came to us from North America in the middle of the 18th century, and was quickly established in cottage gardens, both because of its attraction to bees, and because a pleasant and soothing tea can be made from its leaves.

Bindweed (convolvulus arvensis)

One of the gardeners' nightmare plants – a weed in the fullest sense of the word. To add to its bad reputation, all parts of the plant are poisonous, and it contains a chemical which causes hallucinations. Let's move on quickly.

Biting Stonecrop (sedum acre)

Rejoices in the vernacular name of "welcome-home-husband-though-never-so-drunk," and if you can say that without slurring you must be stone cold sober. How or why this modest little sedum ever came up with such a name defies explanation, since it grows demurely on downland, drystone walls and roofs. It does have a very sharp taste, which is why it was also called wall-pepper, and it used to be given, mixed with vinegar, as *a remedy against poisons inwardly taken*. Perhaps the drunken husband was denied his bed until he'd swallowed a dose of it, which would certainly encourage sobriety.

Blackberry (bramble — rubus macropetalus)

When the common lands were being enclosed at the end of the middle ages, a wide strip was ploughed around the new field in which brambles, hazel, whitethorn and wild roses were planted. This had the double advantage of producing a cattle-proof hedge and a supply of fruit and nuts in the autumn. Picking succulent blackberries, rich in vitamin C, is one of the pleasures of autumn, but it must stop on 29th September, St Michaels Day. This is because, when Satan was unceremoniously bundled out of heaven, he fell into a blackberry bush and departed spitting and cursing (well you would, wouldn't you). Fruit picked after that date was irredeemably spoilt by this ill-tempered behaviour. It is, indeed, the case that by October the zest, as it were, has gone from the blackberry as the damper, foggier new month sets in. The fruit was also seen as a remedy for sores in the mouth and other ulcers, and it was said that young bramble leaves, picked in the spring, could be boiled and used to freshen the complexion.

Bleeding heart (dicentra spectabilis)

Was introduced to Britain from North America in 1846 and thus, being a relative newcomer, had the good fortune to escape the attentions of Tusser, Culpeper and their ilk. Like the peony, it is one of the few plants that thoroughly dislikes being moved once planted, and is liable to go into a prolonged, if not eternal, sulk if you attempt it. It has narcotic properties, and has been used to give relief to menstrual cramps and venereal disease.

Borage (borago officianalis)

In its time, Borage has been regarded as an antidote to bites and stings, ringworm and yellow jaundice and even as a cure for young ladies overindulgent in matters of swooning and unrequited love. Impressive enough, but better still *the leaves and flowers of borage put into wine make men and women glad and merry and drive away all sadness*. Not for nothing was its popular name "cool-tankard," because borage flowers contain potassium nitrate, a soluble crystalline salt that has cooling properties and therefore adds a cool flavour to many kinds of drink. Roman soldiers put it in their beer and wine before battle to keep their spirits up. Until recent times we used it to make cordials, and these days its leaves or flowers are, as a matter of course, used as a garnish for Pimms. Its leaves can also be cooked and eaten like spinach, it's helpful in treating colds and bronchitis, but we seem to have abandoned its use for relieving unrequited love, which seems a pity. On top of all that, it's a pretty flower which brightens up a border and, although it seeds itself with abandon in its quest to help swooning young ladies, it's easy to pull up the excess you don't want.

Butchers Broom (ruscus aculiatus)

You may never have heard of this plant, and you will only find it if you are walking in ancient woodlands, its presence being a sign that the ground has been undisturbed for a long period. At a distant glance it looks like a small holly bush, perhaps 45 cm high, but on closer inspection you'll find its small leaves are an even darker green than those of the holly, and that they are sharp, almost diamond-shaped and very rigid. This is what gives it its name, because butchers used to use a sprig of this tough plant as a brush to scour their wooden chopping blocks. Another, and much prettier, plant which is also a sign of undisturbed woodlands is *yellow archangel*, unflatteringly called "weasel-snout" because of the shape of its flowers. It's a member of the *lamia* family, and looks like a dead nettle, but there are few more attractive sights than a bank of these yellow flowers on a sunny June day.

Carnations (dianthus caryophyllus)

Carnations have been a popular cottage plant for many centuries, and have had a popular association with weddings for much of that time. Being regarded as an aphrodisiac, the flowers were once used to spice the wine given to the bride. Did they seriously believe she needed encouragement? Whatever the truth of it, in Italy the carnation is still the symbol of ardent love, and in Britain it is the flower most commonly found in the buttonhole at a wedding.

> SOON WILL THE HIGH MIDSUMMER POMPS COME ON,
> SOON WILL THE MUSK CARNATIONS BREAK AND SWELL,
> SOON SHALL WE HAVE GOLD-DUSTED SNAPDRAGON,
> SWEET WILLIAM WITH ITS HOMELY COTTAGE SMELL
> AND STOCKS IN FRAGRANT BLOW.
>
> *MATTHEW ARNOLD*

Carrots (daucus carota)

Were also seen as an aphrodisiac by the Tudors, *serving for love matters* as Gerard put it with seemly delicacy, although he would have felt foolish sporting a carrot in his buttonhole at a wedding. Wild carrots have been favoured from antiquity, and thought an excellent aid for healing wounds, especially those resulting from operations to remove gallstones. It has also been believed for a long time that raw carrots improve the eyesight and, although there is some evidence for this, the propaganda put about in the Second World War that British night-fighter pilots ate them to improve their prowess seems rather to have been a cunning ploy to disguise the presence of radar. The opposition would certainly have preferred to face a thin red line of carrots than a battery of radar installations.

Celandine (greater — chelidonium majus, and lesser — ranunculus fiscaria)

The greater and lesser celandines are distinctly different plants, and in no way related. The greater belongs to the poppy family and has a respectable history in country medicine as its various common names suggest — kill-wart, wart-wort and wart-plant being among them ("wort" is the old English name for "plant" or "root"). As these names imply, the acrid orange latex produced when the stem is cut was used to remove warts and corns. The leaves used also to be chewed as a liver tonic and to relieve toothache.

The lesser celandine is related to the buttercup, and was once called pile-wort for reasons that are probably obvious. With that kind of reputation, its customers demanded fairly instant relief and, failing to supply it, the lesser celandine was forced to eke out a modest living half way between that of a weed and a rock plant. Wordsworth, who at the sight of any flower was apt to rush home and dash off a verse, awarded it fifteen minutes of fame:

> There is a flower, the lesser celandine, that shrinks like many more from
>   cold and rain,
> and, the first moment that the sum may shine, bright as the sun himself
>   is out again.

It may not be much, but it's better than being used as a cure for piles.

Celery (apium graveolens)

The Romans were pretty enthusiastic about celery, but it was not one of the things they included in their travelling kit when they settled in Britain, and it didn't turn up here until the 16th century. A hundred years later, John Evelyn waxed lyrical in its praise, liking both the leaves and the stems which, *first peel'd and slit long wise, are eaten with oyl, vinegar, salt and peper... and ever placed in the middle at our Great Men's Tables and Feasts as the grace of the whole board.* The green tops of celery have tended to fall out of favour, which is a pity because they are even fuller of vitamins and minerals than the stems, and if you dry the leaves you can use them in stews, as they used to do, to provide a delicious flavour.

Chamomile (chamaemelum nobile)

The leaves of this small herb have a delicious scent when trodden on or crushed, reminiscent of apples, and therefore make a wonderful plant to grow between the paving-slabs, or as a lawn or, as beloved of the first Elizabethans, a seat. In the days before wardrobes, when clothes were folded and kept in a chest, chamomile and lavender flowers were placed among them to keep them sweet and fresh-smelling. It is still used by some as a relief for migraines or gastric upsets, and it is also said to calm the nervous system of those, highwaymen apart, who are highly strung. Camomile tea is still frequently drunk and although, in the popular imagination, it is fit only for maiden aunts and those likely to encounter Miss Marple on a regular basis, it has made a strong comeback as herbal teas and tissanes have grown in popularity.

Chicory (chicorium intybus)

Was regarded as a laxative in the middle ages, but the good old Tudors refined this a little further. Since it had *vertue to coole the hot burning of the liver, and help the yellow jaundice*, it came to be regarded as a digestive aid when its roots were boiled in broth. Better still, according to a book called *Dry Dinner* in 1599, *the body anoynted with the juyce of chicory is very available to obtaine the favour of great persons!* So if you're planning on going to ask for a salary increase, you know what to do.

Comfrey (symphitum officianale)

Whenever you see "officianale" or "officianalis" in a plant's botanical name you are on to a good thing. It indicates a pedigree established in the monastic physic garden and indicates a herb prized for its healing qualities. Comfrey had several traditional names – Knitbone, Boneset and Saracens Root – giving a strong hint of its particular value. The moistened, pulped root of comfrey was applied to a broken limb, on which it set like plaster, hastening the knitting of the bone. It is said this knowledge was brought back to England by soldiers returning from the Crusades, hence the name Saracens Root, although they didn't know that the reaon for its efficacy is that it contains allantoin, which is valuable for healing connective tissue. Even today, comfrey is used as a poultice for sprains, bruises and abrasions. It is also rich in potassium and, as with nettles, if you leave a bagful to rot in a bucket of rain water for a month it can be used as an excellent liquid feed in the garden, and is especially appreciated by tomatoes. But be warned – nettles or comfrey, it'll smell rotten by the time you come to use it!

Cowslip (primula veris)

Although you may shudder at the thought of despoiling so well-loved a flower, cowslip tea was drunk to soothe headaches and nervous tension, and to counteract insomnia. Cowslip wine is pretty good too.

Daisy (bellis perennis)

The old name for the common or garden (and it's both of these) daisy was days-eye, because it has a golden eye surrounded by white petals which close at dusk and reopen in the morning. Poets have stood in orderly queues to pay homage to it. Inevitably, Wordsworth found himself rushing home to dash off another verse, fearing to be omitted from the company of Milton, Shakespeare, Chaucer and a few of the lesser-known poet laureates. The daisy is one of those unstoppable little plants that turns up everywhere. Quite how it manages to colonise the best bits of the smartest lawns, or the dead centre of a cricket pitch cared for by a small army of groundsmen remains one of life's minor mysteries. But – and it's a big but – it's one of the great homeopathic remedies, its traditional name being *bruisewort*. The flowers and leaves of the daisy contain quantities of oil and ammoniacal salts, and a poultice of leaves is considered excellent for treating bumps and bruises. If you stamp on the leaves and press them to a bruise or swelling, it will respond quickly and well, which is a useful tip for the avid gardener. It works!

> WHEN DAISIES PIED AND VIOLETS BLUE
> AND LADY-SMOCKS ALL SILVER WHITE
> AND CUCKOO-BUDS OF YELLOW HUE
> DO PAINT THE MEADOWS WITH DELIGHT
>
> *SHAKESPEARE*

Dandelion (taraxacum officianale)

The name comes from the French *dent de lion*, lion's tooth, because of the shape of the leaves, and its common name in French is *pissenlit*. In case you've forgotten your school French, its traditional names in English include Pissy beds, Tiddle-beds and Wet-the-bed! Not a well brought up plant at all, but nevertheless an excellent diuretic for flushing out the kidneys and urinary system (as modern science has confirmed), which is why earlier generations, given to a no-nonsense approach, saddled it with its popular names. In every way it's an excellent tonic, which seems to give the blood system a good old cleansing. It has even more going for it than this alone. In the 19th century it was popular in salads, and was a customary filling in sandwiches at genteel afternoon tea parties. Today, chefs on both sides of the Channel, and both sides of the Atlantic make use of it in new ways in, for example, such dishes as dandelion pasta or dandelion and mozarella pie.

Feverfew (tanacetum parthenium)

This is a plant that has had pride of place in herb gardens for two thousand years. Although the Romans brought it to Britain in between bouts of building everything in straight lines, the name is from the old French "febrifuge" meaning to drive away fever, and that is exactly what the monks used it for. It was taken as a cold cure mixed with honey, or used as a gargle for sore throats. Later on it was believed that pushing some feverfew leaves up your nose would help cure a migraine, and since modern science has made so little progress in the matter, maybe it's still worth a shot. Apart from its herbal uses, feverfew is a pretty plant and has been grown in the garden for its flowers since the 16th century.

Later, the Victorians began to cultivate varieties for bedding and today you can choose dwarf varieties for the rock garden or larger ones for herbaceous beds.

Foxglove (digitalis purpurea)

In his *Herball*, Gerard recommended foxglove as a cure for *falling sickness, fevers, agues, liver complaints, suppurating wounds and cleaning the body of naughty humours*, which is a lot to live up to. He was half right, in the sense that folk medicine used infusions of its leaves as a diuretic, and for sore throats and catarrh, but it's a dangerous plant to mess about with because it is highly toxic. The 18th century physician, William Withering, is the person credited with uncovering its greatest benefit, realising that small but accurate quantities of the dried leaf slowed the heartbeat and stimulated the kidneys and lungs. From this, digitalis, came digitoxin and digoxin which modern medicine uses as a heart stimulant. Perhaps the foxglove's powerful toxins persuaded our distant ancestors that it was a plant that fairies lived in, and therefore not one to be picked and brought indoors lest the evil spirits came with it. You will have to make your own mind up about that, but left to grow in the garden it's a plant that spreads a protective leaf or two around its neighbours and helps them to thrive.

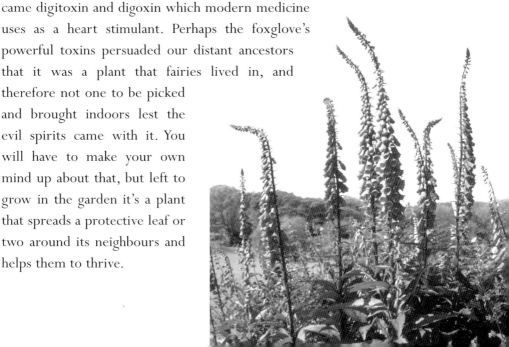

Garlic (allium sativum)

One of the strongest antibiotics in nature, and the most beneficial for human health. There is a price, as Harrington's *English Doctor* noted:

Since garlicke then hath power to save from death,
beare with it though it makes unsavory breath;
And scorn not garlicke, like to some that think
it onely makes men winke, and drinke, and stinke.

The price is well worth paying, however, because garlic lowers blood pressure, helps with lung problems and eases coughs and sore throats. As we already know, it helps to protect both flowers and (some) vegetables in the garden and, as British cooking became steadily more adventurous through the last third of the twentieth century, cooks and chefs the length of the land wouldn't be found in their kitchens without it.

Henbane (hypocamus niger)

Most definitely one to avoid, notwithstanding its use – in minute quantities – in a great many modern medicines (hyoscine, for instance, is used by women in childbirth and those suffering from nervous disorders). Henbane is extremely poisonous to man, and the root can be mistaken for that of chicory or parsnip, which makes it all a little tricky.

Nevertheless, in the hands of ancient Greeks, monks and careful healers, it has a long history of use as a sedative and pain reliever, especially for toothache and, just as with modern hyoscine, nervous disorders. Some things never change.

Hollyhocks (sidalcea malviflora)

The nectar makes wonderful honey, so hollyhocks were planted near the all-important beehives in the traditional cottage garden. But the tradition doesn't stretch all that far back, since they only arrived from China in the 1830's, illustrating the point that our image of the timeless cottage garden, with its drifts of hollyhocks, is a relatively recent one. Fittingly, a poultice of leaves soothes bee and wasp stings, hopefully not both at the same time, and the hollyhock is a prized medicinal plant for soothing coughs and lung complaints.

Hops (humulus lupulus)

You can never be sure where you'll next come across a wild hop, scrambling its way through hedges, winding round a pole or growing on a river bank. Hops are native plants that have been around for centuries, the name coming from the anglo-saxon word "hoppen," meaning to climb. It was not until the 16th century that hops began to be used in ale-brewing, partly as a preservative and partly to inject the bitter flavour that turned ale into beer. The families from the east end of London, who flocked to Kent a century ago for a hop-picking holiday, boiled the young shoots and ate them like asparagus, little knowing that long before them the Romans were doing something similar. The pedigree of the hop as a medicinal herb was established centuries ago, being used to stimulate the appetite, as a mild pain-killer and as a sedative. Until quite recent times, pillows stuffed with hops were popular on both sides of the atlantic to help insomniacs nod off. Pigeon manure is a good compost for successful hop cultivation and, as we haven't heard from Master Tusser for quite some time, we'll let him in here:

> *For hop ground cold,*
> *Dove doong worth gold.*

I don't really understand him either, but that's Thomas for you.

Horseradish (armoracia rusticana)

Love it with beef or hate it, horseradish root is a time-honoured ingredient of a mustard poultice or plaster. Always eager to please, Culpeper was effusive and, for once, almost accurate:

> *If bruised* (he meant the root) *and laid to a part grieved with the*

sciatica, gout, joint-ache or hard swellings of the spleen and liver, it doth wonderfully help them all.

As usual, Mr C. claimed a greater score of potential cures than he should have, but even today a horseradish poultice is thought to be effective in relieving the pain of rheumatism. If, against all advice, you insist on eating the wretched vegetable, take about an ounce of root, grate it very fine, dampen it with some vinegar and mix it into a little thick cream. That, at any rate, is the traditional way of producing horseradish sauce for the traditional roast beef of Old England, but please don't invite me to share it with you.

Houseleek (sempervivum)

If some mouse, spider, fly, wasp, hornet or other venomous beast has by its bite or sting raised a lump on your flesh, rub the injured part gently with the juice of a houseleek and immediately the pain and the swelling will be assuaged.

This worthy and learned subject of Elizabeth I could have added that it's also handy to have around if you burn yourself, or that in the physic gardens the monks thought the juice of its leaves a remedy for rheumatism and for watering eyes. And that's not all. Grown on the roof it was said to protect your dwelling against lightning strikes (presumably making a connection with the relief given to a burn by rubbing it with juice) and it protected you against witches. In short, the pretty little houseleek packs a formidable punch and seems to be proof against most things. One would like a definition of "venomous beast" before committing oneself wholly to its protection, but it might serve in place of the "no hawkers or circulars" signs that were once so common on garden gates.

Hypericum (St John's Wort — hypericum androsaemum)

St Johns Wort, which has been grown in Britain since at least the 14th century, used also to be known by the old French name "Tutsan," from *tout* and *sain* meaning to heal all. It was used to cure ulcers, internal bleeding, internal and external wounds and old sores. Although old folk wisdom sometimes makes improbably comprehensive claims for the virtues of some of the healing plants, in other cases they were impressively accurate, and this is one of them. Even Culpeper, in a rare fit of modesty, contented himself with saying that St Johns Wort *opens obstructions and dissolves swellings*, and he was on the right track. Today, it's used by homeopaths for abscesses and injuries to the nerves — for example, if you fall heavily on the base of your spine, or shut your fingers in the car door. You can buy hypericum tincture in homeopathic chemists and use it externally on such

injuries by diluting it with lukewarm water in equal measures. One variety of St Johns Wort, *hypericum calycinium*, we now know as Rose of Sharon, a Victorian name dating from 1864, and a plant once beloved of country railway stations.

Hyssop (hyssopus officianalis)

Another honoured herb with "officianalis" in its title, whose use can be traced back to classical antiquity. Gerard recommended hyssop with *Figges, water, honie and rue to help the inflammation of the lungs*, and cottage gardeners grew it prolifically, partly as a medicinal plant for use in treating afflictions of the mouth and throat, and partly because it was attractive to bees. Benedictine monks used it to flavour their celebrated liqueurs, which seems an even greater claim to fame and affection. It's a hardy shrub which grows well in a sunny position.

Lavender (lavandula angustifolia)

We've already seen how highly recommended lavender is in the garden, particularly around roses, for repelling harmful insects whilst attracting bees. We tend to claim proprietary rights by calling it Old English Lavender, despite it coming originally from the mediterranean – although since it has been here since at least the 12th century, perhaps we can begin to think of it as our own. Lavender was primarily thought of as a household plant. Like chamomile, its long-lasting fragrance promoted its benefits when laid amongst folded clothes not just to keep them smelling sweet, but also to deter moths from laying their greedy grubs in them.

Today, you can still buy little muslin bags of dried lavender flowers for hanging in wardrobes. Back in the days of stone or beaten earth floors, when straw or rushes were laid on them to trap the dirt, lavender or ladies bedstraw would be strewn as well as a scent to mask the smell of dirt and rotting food. Moreover,

> *the distilled water of lavender smelt into is a refreshing to them that hath the catalepsie, a light migrain, and to them that have the falling sicknesse and that use to swoune much.*

Lettuce (lactuca sativa)

The Chinese were writing about lettuce in the seventh century BC. The Greek philosopher Aristoxenus watered his lettuce beds with wine, and the early Romans decreed that, if administered in human milk, *the juice of wild lettuce takes away dimness of sight and removes ulcers on the eye*. By the time John Evelyn got around to considering the lettuce nearly two thousand years later, it seemed to him that its greatest benefits were *promoting chastity and conciliating sleep*, presumably under the impression that the faster you nodded off the likelier you were to remain chaste. Poor old Culpeper certainly thought so, declaring that it suppressed *venerous dreams* but, as he'd suffered the misfortune of being engaged to a young woman who was struck by lightning and killed on her way to meet him, he may have had a vested interest in such a belief. The one thing on which everyone seems to have concurred in the course of three millennia is that lettuce are easy to grow and the most succulent of all the salad plants.

Mallow (malva sylvestris)

The leaves of the common mallow were thought to be *good against the stinging of scorpions, bees, wasps and such like*, but the roots were even more useful, because they could be turned into a soothing ointment. Indeed, if you boiled the roots and mixed the juice with bread, it made an excellent poultice for wrapping round boils.

(Pot) Marigold (calendula officianalis)

Calendula was another of those plants considered by the old herbalists as a cure for all ills – jaundice, toothache, bee stings and warts to name a few. This may be overstating the case a trifle, but calendula is nevertheless a remarkable plant, and a major weapon in the armoury of the modern homeopathic doctor, by whom it is regarded as the remedy excelling all others for healing open cuts without resort to stitching. Since it cleans the wound as well as repairing it, it's a wonderful thing to have handy, especially with active children liable at any moment to graze a knee on steps or gravel. Luckily tubes of calendula ointment can be bought from many chemists, and if you have occasion to use it, you may well be amazed at the speed with which it heals. If you prefer it as a cordial drink, pour a pint of boiling water over two handfuls of leaves and flowers. Quite apart from healing cuts and inflammations, it is good for the heart and circulation.

THE MARIGOLD, THAT GOES TO BED WI' THE SUN, AND WITH HIM RISES WEEPING

SHAKESPEARE

Marjoram (origanum vulgare)

Very good against the wambling of the stomacke said Gerard, with a satisfaction that is almost audible four hundred years later, and if wambling means what you and I suspect it means, he was spot on, because marjoram tea is an excellent standby for stomach disorders, as well as helpful in fighting off colds, chills and sore throats. Gerard also stated that marjoram was useful if you were *given to overmuch sighing*, and since the oil makes a nice tonic if added to a bath, he may have been right again. The Romans used to give bunches of marjoram as a symbol of peace and friendship. What is indisputable is that origano – wild marjoram – is a wonderful flavouring in cooking, much used by chefs the world over. Sweet marjoram *(origanum majorana)* is very closely related, and likewise appreciated for culinary virtues, and it may have been this herb which the Tudors loved to have in their knot gardens so that the trailing cloaks of

walkers there would brush against it, releasing a pleasant scent. Since oregano goes well with pork, it's odd – or maybe obvious! – that pigs are reputed to loathe the plant, giving rise to the ironic country saying *As a pig loves marjoram*, meaning something thoroughly unattractive.

Mint (common- or spear-mint — mentha spicata, peppermint — mentha piperata, apple mint — mentha rotundifolia)

Gerard called mint the herb *whose smell rejoiceth the hearte of man, for which cause they strew it in chambers of recreation and where feasts and banquets are made.* Culpeper threw off all restraints in his excitement and described it as a cure for virtually every known condition, including his favourite threat, *the bitings of mad dogs.* Standing back from this wave of renaissance enthusiasm, it is true that mediaeval monks grew both apple mint which, being mild, they used in cordials for indigestion, and spearmint, which was a cure for headaches. Peppermint was even stronger, and being an anti-spasmodic, was a cottager's standby for dealing not only with colds and chills but pains and cramps, which made it a woman's friend in particular. It has another attraction, this time for gardeners – if you are pottering in the flower beds on a hot day, you may well find yourself the object of intense interest to clouds of little flies, but a handful of peppermint (from which menthol is distilled) rubbed on your face, neck and hands – not forgetting the inside of your ears – is a good repellent. And once you're back in the house, a window box of peppermint at your kitchen window deters them from coming to inspect what you're cooking. But of all the twenty or so different mints, it's spearmint we are most familiar with today, the one we boil with new potatoes and freshly picked peas.

Nettles (urtica urens)

The Romans bought the good old stinging nettle with them. They ate it, and they rubbed it on their skins to ease painful joints, in their case joints that probably felt rusty in the damp, foggy climate to which, grumbling furiously no doubt, they'd been despatched. They knew a good thing when they saw it. Nettle soup is still made in parts of Scotland, and has found its way south onto the menus of some restaurant chefs – not necessarily in soup, but deep fried in purees; with toast and grated cheese in place of spinach, which it exceeds in iron content; as a bed for poached eggs; or even with fromage frais, new potatoes and a sprinkling of nutmeg. As for rubbing it on yourself, there are recorded modern instances of its use in this way to alleviate arthritis, and there is little difference between this and the recent medical practice of using bee stings to reduce the swelling in inflamed joints.

In Jersey, nettle tea was reckoned an excellent remedy for sore throats and any lung condition, such as pleurisy and, being a good diuretic, it helps to relieve high blood pressure. As you will have gathered, cooking or beating nettles breaks the toxin-filled hairs of the nettle before it can pierce the skin, from which it follows that a nettle will sting you if it brushes you lightly, but is harmless if you grasp it tightly. Hence the expression grasping the nettle, which is not dissimilar to saying that fortune favours the bold.

The hairs of the stinging nettle contain histamine and acetylcholine and, on the good homeopathic principle that like treats like, a tincture of urtica urens is an excellent thing to apply if you suffer a bee sting or a first degree burn – for example from a steaming kettle or a hot stove. Needless to say, the secret is in the dilution, so definitely do not try rubbing a nettle leaf on the sting or burn. Rather, buy your little bottle of urtica urens from most good chemists, and keep it handy. Being struck one moonless evening by a rush of the blindingly obvious, Culpeper advised that: *Nettles are so well known they may be found by feeling for them on the darkest night.* If you are foolish enough to try this out, then the leaf of a dock, potato or tomato will ease the sting – if you can find one in the dark. *Nettle out, dock in; dock relieve the nettle sting* as the old reminder put it. Alternatively, you can wait for the sting to stop tingling after 30 minutes or so, and think of all the anti-arthritic good you've just done yourself.

Onion (allium cepa)

If a little less powerfully, onions nevertheless share many of garlic's antiseptic properties. They have a deserved reputation for helping to ward off infectious diseases and, boiled in milk, are a good remedy for colds – though you may have to decide which of these two evils is the lesser. In the old days there was a widespread habit of hanging strings of onions in the house to keep it free of infectious diseases because, it was believed, onions absorbed poisons. Gerard had a cunning ruse up his capacious sleeve. He reckoned that *the juice of onions annointed on a bald head in the sun, bringeth the haire again very speedily*, but if this were true it seems unlikely the world would still be so full of shining pates. Gerard's proposal may have increased cases of Elizabethan sunstroke, but a reversal of depilation seems at the best unproven. But if you're desperate...

Pansy (heartsease — viola)

Pansies belong to the viola family and are a much-loved and modest flower of which Mary Shelley wrote: *The pansy, heartsease, let my flower be.* In the wild, before plant breeders had their wicked way with it and transformed it into a range of colours and sizes, it was a uniformly dull yellow and was a staple of monastic gardens, being used internally to heal sores and ulcers. It was *good for such as are sick of the ague, especially children and infants.*

Penny-royal (mentha pulegium)

Closely related to the mint family, penny-royal was once upon a time a staple of monastic physic gardens and country medicine. Its latin name gives a clue to one of its uses. "Pules" is a flea, and it was sometimes used as a strewing plant to go on the floor among the rushes with, or instead of, lavender or chamomile as a means of counteracting the bad effects of all the dirt and insects lurking underfoot. Its main use, however, was as a sedative and antispasmodic which is, perhaps, why the Romans thought of it as preventing sea sickness. Good old Gerard came up with the bright suggestion that *a garland of pennie royall worne about the head is of great force against the swimming in the head.* In one bound he went from sea sickness to head-swimming — though you can see how he got there. The sad thing is that this sweet-smelling and attractive little plant has now become so uncommon in Britain that it is almost endangered.

Peony (paeonia officianalis)

Peonies have been grown here since well before the Battle of Hastings, taking their name from the Greek physician Paeon. As its "officianalis" tag conveys, it was grown in the kitchen and physic gardens of monasteries and nunneries, the seeds being used to flavour meat and, steeped in wine, as *a speciall remedie for those that are troubled with night Mare*, though whether it was the wine or the seeds that did the trick was kept secret. It was, to be fair to the monks, the seeds or even the dried and ground root, which was a recognised anti-spasmodic used in the treatment of nervous afflictions, childbirth and epilepsy. Its sumptuous flowers were an incidental by-product to our ancestors, but our main reason for continuing to welcome it in our gardens a millennium later.

Radish (raphanus sativus)

The ancient Egyptians, the classical Greeks and the conquering Romans were all big consumers of radishes, though they didn't necessarily admit to actually *liking* them. *A vulgar article of diet* growled Pliny. Still, the radish was credited with being one of the plants of Mars, and Evelyn believed it might be helpful in *repelling the vapours of wine*, whilst his contemporaries assured their reading public that they *drive the stone out of the kidneys and bladder*. Since being cut for the stone was one of the most frightening things you might face back in the days of Sam Pepys, you could understand people grasping at any straw or, in this case, radish. Even more optimistically, they were said to cure corns on the feet, but only if they were cut when the moon was waning. You might employ your time better by eating them whilst you wait for the moon to wane.

Rhubarb (rheum rhabarbarum)

Rhubarb is included mainly as a warning. Because rhubarb is a fruit many people have come to like, albeit only in the 19th century, it is tempting to make use of the leaves. Please don't do it. They are poisonous, and whilst the early Victorians were experimenting with the plant, a few people died from doing just that. The stem, of course, is a different matter. It is full of oxalic acid and, quite apart from being wonderful with custard or in a crumble, it makes excellent wine.

Rosebay willow-herb (epilobium angustifolium)

Whilst it would be wrong to call the rosebay willow-herb rare in the 19th century, it is one of those plants that bucked the 20th century trend to push our wild flowers to the margins. In the USA it is called fireweed, which gives the first clue why this is so. It has a liking for ground that has been cleared by fire or other means, and it was the devastation resulting from two world wars that gave the rosebay willow-herb its chance to proliferate. WWI saw huge tracts of woodland cut down, and the bombing of cities in WWII created ideal conditions in which the feathery, airborne seeds could mount an aerial invasion with every chance of landing in a promising spot. A small case of good coming out of bad.

Rosemary (rosemarinus officianalis)

The very name brings enchantment – *ros maris*, meaning dew of the sea – and it is another of the "officianalis" plants beloved of the monasteries. Distilled oil was obtained from rosemary and used as a perfume, and is still one of the ingredients of eau de cologne. It was also credited with improving the memory and being good for the head. In his *Herball*, Gerard said:

> *It comforteth the cold, weak and feeble brain in a most wonderful manner*

which may explain why the most prominent people in ancient Rome were prone to wandering the streets with garlands of rosemary around their necks. For country folk busy with the day to day problems of eking out a living the concerns of their stomachs ranked well above those of their hair or heads. For them, as for us today, rosemary added flavour to meats such as mutton, rabbit and poultry and, an important consideration, it kept witches at bay – of which more later.

FOR YOU THERE'S ROSEMARY AND RUE;
THESE KEEP SEEMING AND SAVOUR ALL THE WINTER LONG

SHAKESPEARE

Roses (rosa)

Whenever the red rose of England appears as a symbol, whether on the shirts of the England rugby XV or on a political platform, it's the modern, cultivated rose that's depicted, but the true heraldic flower is the wild, or dog, rose (*rosa canina*). The 15th century Wars of the Roses were so-called because each side adopted a rose as its symbol – and you can still grow a rose called *white rose of york*, which is close to the one the Yorkists knew, and a red one called *apothecary's rose*, which the Lancastrians might have recognised. The oldest rose of all, though, is the damask rose, which goes back at least four thousand years and from which comes Attar of Roses.

MID-MAY'S ELDEST CHILD, THE COMING MUSK-ROSE,
FULL OF DEWY WINE

KEATS

In the monastic gardens of England, they cultivated both white and red roses. The red rose was rosa *gallica officianalis*, and among its many medicinal uses was that of staunching bleeding, whilst the white rose, *rosa alba maxima*, was prized as a distillation which helped the heart. Rose-hips, or itchy-coos as they were known in some parts, have a long history as a food. Gerard approved of them in *most pleasant meates and banketting dishes, as tartes and such like*, and then, in the 1930's, scientists discovered that the hips of the wild dog rose contain a higher concentration of vitamin C than just about any other fruit or vegetable. It would take forty oranges to overhaul the value of a single cupful of rose hip juice, and since oranges were none too easy to come by during World War II, it comes as no surprise that an entire generation of wartime children was brought up on rose hip syrup. Over 450 tons of rose hips were gathered in the last year of the war. And why the popular name itchy-coos? Easy. It took the kids no time at all to work out that if you dropped a hairy rose hip down the neck of the one in front it made an excellent substitute for itching powder!

Sage (salvia officianalis)

Now for the undisputed star of the show. When you look at those regimental rows of shock-red salvias in the public park, you wouldn't think that you're looking at a distant cousin of a quite remarkable plant, would you?

Why should a man die if he grows sage in his garden?

asked a Roman proverb, and in Britain:

Eat sage in May, and you'll live for aye

is a saying that's been around for a very long time although, even by

American standards of clinging to life by the fingernails, sage can't quite deliver that great a miracle. Indeed, as John Evelyn said in the 17th century, sage seemed to have so many remarkable properties he wondered only that man was not yet immortal.

The name *salvia* comes form the latin "salvere" meaning to make safe or well, and its particular uses in the physic gardens were to cleanse the blood and promote female fertility – *to help women better forward in their child-bearing* as Parkinson put it. Sage is an antiseptic and astringent, and its leaves have also been used with apparent success to treat headaches and colds, liver complaints, lethargy and aching muscles, and epilepsy. Like some other plants that sidle protectively up to human beings, it's unpopular in the insect world. If, for example, you're working in the garden on a summer's evening and the gnats and midges are proving troublesome, try sticking some sprigs of sage in your clothes and behind your ears, and they'll probably leave you in peace.

We're not done with sage because, whilst there are other plants that can at least challenge it's many healing properties, there are few, if any, that are genuinely good to eat and drink as well. Sage beer was very popular in Tudor and Elizabethan times, as were sage leaves when fried in batter. It's a great aromatic herb for use in flavouring soups, salads, cheeses, desserts, wines and liqueurs (and very familiar today in sage and onion stuffing for the turkey). And in Greece, you can still wander into a café and order a sage tea.

We still haven't finished with sage. Its relative, wild clary (*salvia verbenaca*) has been used as a wash for sore eyes since mediaeval times, earning itself the nickname "clear-eyes" – clary for short. The seeds were soaked in water until they were like a jelly, and drops were then put in the eye. And on top of all these fine qualities, sage is a beautiful flower to have in the garden.

Self-heal (prunella vulgaris)

It was also called "sicklewort" or "carpenter's herb" because of its use in stemming blood after accidents. A common wild flower, it was dried and powdered and applied externally and, as the common names suggest, the kind of thing a man would probably have carried with him if he was working with sharp tools.

Solomons Seal (polygonatum biflorum)

Another herb for healing wounds and broken bones which, according to mediaeval belief, had been approved by Solomon himself. A little like comfrey, the root needed to be pulped and applied to the wound like a poultice, when it *knitteth the joynt very firmly*. But Gerard also said of it that *it taketh away in one night or two at the most, any bruise, black or blue spots gotten by falls or womens' wilfulness, stumbling upon their hasty husband's fist or suchlike*. We had better move on.

Sorrel (rumex acetosa)

Sorrel, which is very common in the fields in the second half of summer, used to be called all sorts of unflattering names – sour dogs, sour sops, vinegar plant being just a few – but it's not really as bad as that. It is sharp and astringent, certainly, but very refreshing, and workers in the fields would chew the raw leaves to slake their thirst. Before the days of lemons, sorrel was used to flavour food, fish particularly, as it still is, and now is increasingly found in salads, soups and sauces.

Wild strawberry (fragaria vesca)

The leaves and berries of wild strawberries were used to ease painful gums and inflamed wounds, whilst the distilled juice was said to remove spots and make the face "fair and smooth." Drunk with white wine, it was recommended for reviving the spirits. Isn't it odd how many herbs are credited with reviving the spirits provided they are mixed with wine! Worse was to come. According to Andrew Boorde, born well before the invention of lawn tennis, but evidently with the gift of clairvoyance: *raw creame undecocted, eaten with strawberys, hath put men in jeopardy of their lives.* Alter "lives" to "bank balances" and you have a description of summer-time Wimbledon.

Thyme (common – thymus vulgaris; wild – thymus polytrichus; lemon – thymus citriodus)

Thyme is a natural antiseptic, and this is one of the reasons it's a country workhorse. Medicinally, both wild and common thyme were used for sore throats, lung complaints and gastric upsets, and to relieve *the melancholicke and troubled in spirit and mind*. In the middle ages it helped you to see fairies which, as they were mainly evil in intent, probably brought on a melancholicke fit creating, therefore, something of a vicious circle. Its other great use, then as now, was in cooking and it was used with fatty meats, as well as in soups and stuffing, where its antiseptic properties helped to counteract the effects of the fat content.

Violets (violaceae)

One of the reasons violets are regarded as country flowers is that they need clean air to flourish and are therefore not commonly found in the middle of cities or towns. They have nevertheless been cultivated for over two thousand years, and in the monasteries a syrup made from violets was used to flavour omelettes and custards. It was a flower that helped you to sleep, though you had to take extreme measures to achieve this blissful state, at least according to the herbalist Anthony Ascham:

Seep this herb in water and at eventide let him soak well his feet in the water to the ankles, and he shall sleep well.

Wallflower (erysimum cheiri)

Wallflowers, known of old as the March or winter gillyflower, have been very popular in cottage gardens for many generations, growing particularly well (as the name implies) in crevices in dry walls. Today, we're most familiar with the biennial variety, but the perennial wallflower has staged a comeback in popularity and it will flower annually, the only snag being that it is not long-lived. Three or four years and it's given up on you, so you need either to encourage them to seed and spread, or bring in new ones fairly frequently. It had its place in the monastic order of things, and was used to cure ulcers of the mouth if boiled with wine, honey and allom, or made into an oil which, as Gerard assured his groaning sufferers, *is good to be used to anoint a goutie part.*

THE FAIREST FLOWERS O' THE SEASON
ARE OUR CARNATIONS AND STREAKED GILLYVORS
WHICH SOME CALL NATURE'S BASTARDS

SHAKESPEARE

Yarrow (achillea)

The many forms of achillea now available make it a beautiful plant in the right place or, in its common form in the wrong place, a pestilential weed. It was named after Achilles, hero of the Trojan wars, who was reputed to have bound his soldiers' wounds with yarrow to stop the bleeding. As a result it acquired such popular names as "soldiers woundwort" and "staunch- weed." Research has established that yarrow does indeed contain blood-clotting chemicals, which is why gardeners hung a few handfuls of yarrow leaves in the tool shed, and would sometimes bind it round the handles of their tools in case of cuts. An infusion of yarrow induces sweating, which made it a good thing to take if you were fighting the 'flu or a heavy cold. And it's another of those plants that protects its fellows, and lends a helping root to those around it. So maybe you shouldn't curse the common bit growing in the "wrong" place after all! Finally, it's another plant recommended to replace your lost hair with luxuriant growth!

Protection against lightning strike...

Although Culpeper seemed convinced that the greatest hazard of life was the bitings of mad dogs, fire, lightning and witchcraft were the things our more distant ancestors really feared. Fear of lightning was understandable when you lived in a world made almost entirely of wood, so you needed around you those plants said to have the necessary protective aura:

> *Elder, Hazel, Rowan and Walnut trees;*
> *Holly and Bay or Laurel;*
> *Houseleek and Mistletoe.*

...and against witchcraft

So many things which might mean the difference between ease and suffering, or even life and death, could go wrong that it did not seem fanciful to believe malign spirits were at hand. Our modern equivalent of a broomful of witches in the garden is probably finding the tabloid press or a politician on the doorstep. Try these to be rid of them:

> *Blackberry, holly, juniper and rosemary;*
> *Fennel, garlic, mullein and rue;*
> *Broom, houseleek and snapdragons (antirrhinum).*

Good luck!

Master Tusser has stayed commendably quiet for a while, so he can write the epilogue for this chapter:

> *Thus ends in breefe, of herbes the cheefe,*
> *to get more skill, read whom ye will.*

DON'T BUG ME –
I'M ON YOUR SIDE

BIRDS, INSECTS AND OTHER PESTS AND FRIENDS

The worst enemyes to gardens are moles, catts, earewiggs, snailes and mice, and they must be carefully destroyed, or all your labor is lost, said Sir Thomas Hanmer in 1589. Cat lovers will be outraged at such profanity of an animal the Egyptians regarded as a god. The fact remains the cat is a mixed blessing. A fat, lazy cat dozing centre stage on the lawn will certainly deter birds intent on getting to your fruit or cabbages before you do, but it will just as effectively frighten away those that do a sterling job in minimising the vast population of slugs, snails and greenfly that do much more extensive damage. As Joseph Addison wrote three hundred years ago:

> *I value my garden more for being full of blackbirds than of cherries,
> and very frankly give them fruit for their songs.*

The brutal fact is that cats kill a frightening number of birds and small mammals without accounting for a single slug or snail. The choice is yours – and that's quite enough about cats!

Crows have always ranked high in the countryman's consciousness, but with ambivalent feelings. They are in truth the Al Capones of the bird world, bullying other birds and stealing their eggs. The irony is that if crows encounter a buzzard, an owl in the daytime, or any bird they think resembles a bird of prey, they rise in a swarm and mob it mercilessly. In fact, neither buzzard nor owl attacks other birds. The sparrow hawk is quite another matter. It will spot a small bird taking refuge in a tree, glide silently around to the back of the tree and then, with a rapid dive and a squawk, emerge with its supper.

As the presence of scarecrows suggests, crows were the robbers of seed as well as of other birds' eggs. *Scare away crowes, good sonne, see fencing be done* warned our old friend Thomas Tusser. As we saw earlier, you were advised, when sowing, to *sow one for the rook and one for the crow, one to die and one to grow*. In other words the crow family were going to account for 50% of your would-be crop. On the other hand there was a saying that: *Rooks only build where there's money*, betraying a contrary superstition that prosperity visited the places where rooks (one of eight members of the crow family) nested.

In country lore, the flight of crows was an indicator of the next day's weather. If the crows were seen returning high in the sky to their nests

after a hard day's work stealing your seeds, the weather was set fair for the next twenty-four hours. Conversely, a low flight-path foretold wet weather. *As the crow flies* suggests the shortest route between two points, in the belief that crows (only the rook branch of the family, in fact) always took the quickest way home.

Perhaps because crows, together with their fellow family-members, magpies, are the most commonly seen birds in the countryside, there are myriad rhymes foretelling fortune featuring one or other of the birds. Typical of them is:

One crow sorrow
Two crows joy
Three crows a girl
Four crows a boy
Five crows silver
Six crows gold
Seven crows a secret never to be told.

Most variations agree that a single crow is a bad omen, and two a promise of happiness, but the differences attached to other numbers can involve heaven, hell, marriage, birth and so on.

The other bird of particular note in the countryman's consciousness was a migrating bird, the cuckoo. The reasons are obvious enough because, whilst many migrating birds return in the spring, the cuckoo has an insistent and unmistakable call to register its presence and its territory. Even today, many people keep an ear cocked to record the earliest call of the cuckoo but as a general rule it was reckoned that 14th April, St Tibertius' Day, signalled the start of the cuckoo season.

Turn your money when you hear the cuckoo and you'll have money in your purse till he come again went one piece of advice, which relied on spring having sprung, as it were, on time. In this event, the grass would be growing well and the cattle and sheep would have plenty to eat when they were put out to graze. It was a different matter if spring was late and the trees were yet to show any growth. If this were the case it was better to invest your money in seed rather than livestock:

When the cuckoo comes to the bare thorn
sell your cow and buy your corn.

It would be wrong to say that country lore ignores other birds but, in the days when woodland and meadow were more plentiful than they are now, they had space to go about their business without becoming too entangled with man's agricultural efforts. There were occasional observations – for example, the arrival of fieldfares (a member of the thrush family) in the garden was said to signal imminent snow; the gathering of swallows in the trees told you, supposing you were not fully aware of the fact already, that autumn was coming (these days, of course, the migrating swallows find British Telecoms' telegraph lines a much more sociable departure lounge as they check their passports and prepare to leave the country).

Of all the insect life going on around country farms and cottages, that of the bee was of the greatest interest and concern. Honey, which was, after all, the only sweetener available until cane sugar began to be imported less than three hundred years ago, was sometimes used in lieu of money, whilst beeswax was if anything even more valuable, providing not only the best source of lighting if made into candles but also a healing ointment for treating wounds thanks to the resin called propolis that it contained.

And Before Him in the Sunshine Passed the Bees,
The Honey-Makers, Burning, Singing in the Sunshine

LONGFELLOW

If a swarm of bees settled in the thatch of your cottage it was, therefore, very good news indeed, and little wonder that Thomas Tusser's brow wrinkled with anxiety on your behalf – *Good dwelling give bee or hence goes shee*, he urged. It was one thing for the swarm to visit you, but you then had to claim ownership. Even in pre-Christian times, the advice for this was clear: take some earth and sprinkle it with the right hand under the right foot crying "I hold it under foot; I have found it." That done, you must throw a handful of earth or grit over the swarm, saying "Stay, victorious women, sink to earth. Never fly wild to the wood." Superstition cloaks a sound reason for this action. If danger, such as a hailstorm, threatens the swarm it will cluster tightly around the queen and bring her safely to the ground so, having claimed ownership, you could then take physical possession of the swarm, which could only be done once it was within reach at ground level.

Naturally enough, the season of the year determined the value of your good fortune, hence:

A swarm of bees in May is worth a load of hay
A swarm of bees in June is worth a silver spoon, but
A swarm of bees in July is not worth a fly.

Given their value, and the sheer chance by which they had come into your ownership, it is not surprising that a good deal of superstition lingered around bees. One of the strongest beliefs was that they must always be informed of a death in the family, and most especially of that of the head of the household, their nominal owner. If they were not, they might fly off and the family's good fortune would be at an end.

The poor master's dead, but you must work for me

was typical of the form in which the news was to be delivered to the bees – sometimes as the funeral cortege left the house, sometimes in the middle of the night, but nearly always stressing the new ownership. Similarly, the bees must be told of other major events, such as a marriage, and if they continued to hum it showed they had accepted the news. If, on the other hand, the household was an unhappy or argumentative one, the bees would not do well, and might even leave you for more congenial surroundings.

A further belief was that the owner of the hive should visit the bees to consult them about his day's work, though this was merely a way of acknowledging that they were useful short-term weather forecasters –

If the bees stay at home, rain will soon come;
If they fly away, fine will be the day.

Since bees depended on open flowers for their supply of nectar and pollen, it is scarcely remarkable that they stayed in bed in wet weather.

Elsewhere in the garden, folk had learned by experience and practice how to make use of plants with insect-repelling qualities to protect those that lacked them, as we've already seen with garlic, lavender, marigolds, foxgloves and the like. It was necessary also to know which insects were on your side, and therefore to be encouraged.

Spiders were generally well thought of, partly for the sterling work they do controlling pests such as flies, aphids and woodlice in the garden, and partly for their dogged persistence in hunting flies indoors. In some cultures, indeed, spiders were regarded as sacred but, more prosaically, the British merely thought of them as bringers of luck and prosperity: *If you wish to live and thrive, let the spiders run and live* was an old saying, and you will still find people who will tell you that *when big hairy spiders come into the house, autumn's arrived and they must be left alone.*

Odd though it sounds it used to be said that, to ward off whooping cough, you should put a spider in a bag round your neck (not as odd, to be sure, as the dire "cure" of mouse pie for bed-wetting, though perhaps the threat was considered more efficacious than the pie!) Spiders' webs were considered useful for wrapping round small cuts or wounds to stop the bleeding, and spiders were also a weather reference because, if a storm was threatening, the spider would, as it were, pull in its web, making it more compact to withstand the developing threat to it.

In addition to spiders, there is a longish list of insects, birds and animals that are on your side in the eternal war with the sap-sucking hordes intent on overrunning your flowers, fruit and vegetables, and it's as well to know who they are. Animals can be left for the moment, but on the subject of insects there are out-and-out goodies, and then there are the ones that kick over the traces now and again. They can be good, but they can also be immensely irritating. Take wasps, for example. In the early part of the summer, they're regular Dr Jekylls, feeding on insect pests and caterpillars on our behalf and, later in the year, craneflies; but the minute the fruit begins to ripen, they turn into Mr Hydes. Put bluntly, they become drunk on nectar and, like their human counterparts staggering out of the pub, become obsessed with a single irrational idea – in their case that any picnic involving sweet material, such as jam, honey, lemonade or fruit juice is the only place where it's smart to be seen. If you're one of the lucky majority who is barely affected by a wasp sting, which only contains a little toxin, you won't be too bothered by them. Otherwise, a little jam, honey, sugar or beer in a jar, covered with enough water to drown in, will help to get rid of them. The same solution applies to protecting your fruit from them when it is still on the tree, though in this case it means some hard work hanging the jars with string from the branches.

The earwig is in a similar category. During the summer it slaves away ridding us of mites and the eggs of codling moths, which attack apples, until our dahlias emerge. It's very partial to dahlia flowers, and on the assumption you don't want to cover the dahlia with lethal chemical sprays (which will kill friends as well as enemies), the best you can do is invert a flower pot with a little straw in it on the top of the cane supporting the plant. Some of the earwigs will curl up in the nice warm bed you've provided and, each morning, you can dispose of your earwig collection as you please. But there will always be enough old lags, who've seen it all before and are far too wily to be caught, to keep the earwig population ticking over.

NATURE IS OFTEN HIDDEN, SOMETIMES OVERCOME, SELDOM EXTINGUISHED

SIR FRANCIS BACON

The insects who lead blameless lives and are on your side all summer long include:

Ladybirds — red or yellow, with anything from two to fourteen spots: these members of the beetle family devote six months of the year to feasting on your aphids, mites, mealy bugs, scale insects and caterpillars, and will even help keep mildew at bay.

Beetles: There are many varieties of beetle, and the more you have of them the better for your garden since they demolish slugs, flatworms, vine weevils, root aphids and carrotfly larvae all year round, public holidays included. Of the slightly unusual beetles, you may well encounter a green one, the Green Tiger Beetle, which eats ants and other insects; and the Devil's Coachman or Coach-horse. Unlike most beetles, the latter does not have wing cases over its back and, if it feels threatened, it will swing the rear half of its body up and over, imitating a scorpion. It is harmless and, again, a great destroyer of pests. Unfortunately, many slug pellets contain methiocarb, and this kills beetles as well. Worse, if a bird takes an affected beetle it, too, will probably die.

Harvestmen: These are arachnids, but do not have bodies divided into two sections like normal spiders, nor do they spin webs which would use up time more usefully devoted to hunting down aphids and caterpillars on your behalf. Since they hunt at night, you're most likely to see them in the evening, storming around the garden in a jumble of eight very long, thin legs in the middle of which the tiny body is suspended. Cheer them on their way, because they are good news.

Hoverflies: They disguise themselves to look a little like wasps, which occasionally has unfortunate consequences at human hands. Wait to see if they hover (which a wasp cannot do) and spare the rolled-up newspaper, because they're itching to get in among the aphids, red spider mites and even small caterpillars.

Lacewings: The diet of the lacewing is very similar to that of the hoverfly, and its appearance fairly unmistakable for anything else since the four long wings are delicate and, indeed, like lace. The body can be either green or brown.

Centipedes: They may look insignificant, but they have an insatiable appetite, which they exercise on an unstinting, year-long basis, for the larvae of carrot and cabbage fly, and for slugs and snails.

Bats and Birds: Being creatures of the night, you may not be aware that, while you sleep, bats have mounted night patrol over your garden consuming prodigious quantities of gnats, aphids, moths and other insects. The tiniest of them, the pipistrelle, can eat as many as 3,000 in a night. Likewise, garden birds such as thrushes, blackbirds, wagtails, robins and tits account for barrow-loads of slugs, snails, caterpillars, leatherjackets and aphids. A single pair of blue tits, for example, could need anything from 12,000 to 20,000 caterpillars and grubs for a brood of between six and fifteen chicks.

ALL NATURE SEEMS AT WORK. SLUGS LEAVE THEIR LAIR –
THE BEES ARE STIRRING – BIRDS ARE ON THE WING.

COLERIDGE

Despite the impressive quantities of insects for which your garden friends account there is, nevertheless, one immutable law of nature that not even an army of scientists will ever change, and that is that pests will always outnumber their predators because they breed with greater determination and in greater numbers. For that reason, you need every bit of help you can get and I can only refer you back to pages 51– 60, and the list of plants which offer protection by emitting scents or chemicals which deter or destroy the ill-intentioned insects.

There are one or two more solutions which country folk have found effective:

- Soak a few handfuls of nettles in water (preferably rainwater) for a few days, draw off the liquid through a spray, and use against aphids;

- Alternatively, boil the leaves of wild garlic and use the resulting liquid as a spray for the same purpose.

- Because it contains oxalic acid in quantities that are harmful even to human beings, soak about a pound of rhubarb leaves in two pints of water for roughly a month, and use the liquid to spray fruit trees in leaf (but before the fruit has formed). Be very careful to label the liquid and to keep it well out of the way of children.

- Potatoes that have gone green, perhaps from not being properly earthed up, are poisonous. By boiling half a dozen or so in a medium-sized pan, the water, when drawn off, will make an insect-repellent spray.

- To prevent cabbage root fly and carrot fly, shake a few drops of paraffin into a little dry sand and sprinkle it alongside the plants to deter the insects from laying eggs. You will need to do this little and often, and to renew the mixture after rain;

- As a carrot fly preventative, it's a good idea to crumble a mothball into the seed drill as you sow the carrots, but it needs to be the old-fashioned kind, containing camphor or napthalene, not the modern sort with chemical substitutes;

- Mothballs are also useful in scaring slugs away from your potatoes. Just pop one mothball in with each tuber. It won't harm the tuber, but the slug will look elsewhere;

- Clusters of mothballs (still the old-fashioned sort) hung among the branches have long been a standby against leaf curl in peach trees. It may not look elegant, but they are consistently said to work.

- If you are persecuted by mildew on your cabbages or sprouts, use a solution of methylated spirits and water as a spray;

- Mildew on gooseberry bushes is a common problem, but if you soak a few chives in boiling water for a little while, you can wipe the liquid onto the leaves of the bush to get rid of it;

- And if you've also got a problem with cucumber mildew, take what's left of the anti-aphid concoction of boiled wild garlic leaves and spray it on the cucumbers.

If, despite all the friendly insects crowding these pages, and all the precautions you've taken, you still can't keep the pests down to reasonable proportions, you may need to move house!

NOW YOU SEE THEM; NOW YOU DON'T

THE ANIMALS AROUND US

Man has become so urbanised and egocentric that, unless he finds a fox actually in his dustbin as he gets out of his car, he often fails to realise that all around an endless cycle of hunting, feeding, life and death is being played out between mammals, birds and insects. Our rural ancestors had to be much more observant and aware of it, and the extent to which animals permeate country lore is largely dependent on how close the animals come to daily human life. Broadly speaking, there are the domesticated animals and poultry of the farmyard or smallholder's field, whose purpose is economic; the wild animals that approach the house and garden to hunt; and the animals of forest and field who keep a wary distance.

Throughout the middle ages, the pig was a staple of life, of which every home needed at least one if it could get it, because its flesh could be smoked and preserved for longer than other meats. Indeed, for poor peasants it might well be the only meat available, and so an expression like *bacon brains* became a reference to a simpleton, or someone of low social

standing. Pigs were often given as prizes at fairs or festivals, a favourite competition – which lasted well into the twentieth century – being to catch a greasy pig set loose in the ring. These country prizes gave rise to an expression we still use – *bringing home the bacon* – and at Dunmow in Essex they give a side of bacon, christened the Dunmow Flitch, to the married couple who can prove they haven't quarrelled for a year and a day. The custom is nearly nine hundred years old, yet as recently as the 1960's the names of the winners might be an item on national radio.

Even today, there is a higher density of sheep in Britain than in any country in the world apart from New Zealand. Throughout the middle ages the wool trade was of immense importance to England's economy, and magnificent houses and churches were built with the resultant wealth in its centre, East Anglia, including the "wool cathedral" at Lavenham in Suffolk. So:

> *Shear your sheep in May,*
> *and shear them all away*

was timely advice not to be premature and shear the fleece too early in the year, lest you lose the sheep to exposure. And of course to be the black sheep of the family meant to be the odd one out, usually for reprehensible reasons. Black-faced sheep were not unknown, but their wool was considered less easy to dye, and therefore less valuable. We still refer to someone "woolgathering" when they appear to be lost in thought, and the expression has a long pedigree. Since every strand of wool was important, the less able people on the farm or in the village were given the task of wandering the fields gathering the wool torn from the sheep's coats by the bushes. At a distance this appeared to be an aimless occupation, and became applied to anyone wearing a vacant expression!

From the 18th century onwards, as the population began to climb, sheep became more important as a source of meat than for their wool. The expression *as well be hanged for a sheep as a lamb* came from that period when to be caught stealing a sheep meant the death penalty, a law not revoked until the 19th century. So if you were hungry enough to risk your neck, the gallows humour advised you to run off with an entire sheep rather than a lamb half its size.

Just as most people would hope to keep a pig near the house, so they would wish for geese, or at least a goose, as well. As autumn drew on, the prospect of a long winter with little or no fresh food stretched ahead, and if the slaughtered and smoked pig offered a supply of partially preserved meat, the goose represented the last fresh meat for several months. To cook your goose meant that you were now committed, there was no way back from the course of action just taken, and that, in turn, could be taken to mean plans going awry in a way you would regret. Even so, having cooked the goose there was a liberal supply of fat, and fat had many uses. In mediaeval days, when sanitation was notable only for its absence, it was excellent for body insulation. If you applied a layer of goose fat and then stitched yourself into your clothing, you stood a chance of staying warm in winter. Maybe the 21st century isn't so bad after all.

Hens pecking around the homestead or the farmyard were common enough and, as with many other creatures, an order of precedence existed at meal times. The "cock of the walk" was the cockerel that had fought the other cocks to a standstill over an unspecified number of rounds, to establish first choice of the grain in the yard, or walk. So, too, the hens established hierarchies, and the top hen could cheerfully peck any other hen she felt in the mood to peck without fear of retaliation. Down at the bottom of the heap was, inevitably, a poor old hen who could be pecked by anybody – and usually was. Thus was the pecking order established. As always in nature, it evolved to ensure the survival of the fittest and, therefore, the continuation of a vigorous flock, or pack, or herd. One day, inevitably, the top cock and the top hen would become too old to maintain their supremacy. Then they would go to the bottom of the hierarchy and be pecked, probably to death, by the rest. One feels this would be apt for politicians, which may be why they gave themselves a refuge by inventing life peerages!

We may see little of many animals who visit our gardens because they are either nocturnal or secretive. Hedgehogs are endearing favourites who do us a great service by putting slugs, snails and caterpillars at the top of their menu. It's a pity that they are also partial to earthworms – who perform the vital task of bringing fresh nutrients up to the surface – and, if they can get them, birds' eggs. Hedgehogs have been around, pretty much unaltered, for around 15 million years, longer than homo sapiens is likely to achieve, so their defences against predators are obviously pretty effective – except against foxes, badgers and lorry drivers. If you find a hedgehog skin in a field, it's likely that a fox has taken it, because badgers will leave no trace. The fate of a flat hedgehog in the middle of a road is, alas, all too apparent.

These hazards apart, hedgehogs need very little help from us except in two respects. Please try not to leave an empty tin of, say, baked beans lying around outside. The last little lick at the bottom is irresistible to a hedgehog, but nature didn't design him for crawling into tins and he's liable to get stuck. In October, hedgehogs are putting on body fat in readiness for hibernation so, if you know you have them in the neighbourhood, a saucer of dog or cat food, and a bowl of water (but not bread and milk) will be very much appreciated. If you have a heap of leaves or dead wood, or a bonfire pile, in your garden, please try not to disturb it between November and March in case there are hedgehogs in it. If a hibernating animal is woken, its metabolism begins working again, consuming body fat, and it may then not survive through until spring.

Common shrews much prefer life in woodland and hedgerow but, as they have voracious appetites for insects, slugs, snails and earthworms, they will certainly venture into gardens. Their bite is toxic, which enables them to kill baby mice and, in the extremely unlikely event that you are bitten by one, you will find it a little uncomfortable. Shrews reproduce in huge numbers, with five litters a year and up to seven offspring in each, which is just as well since they are an owl's favourite prey and buzzards and sparrow-hawks will also go for small mammals such as shrews and voles (and will even take earthworms). Consequently, shrews take care to keep under cover of grass, leaves and roots, so you may see little or nothing of them. Shrews give off a musky odour, which may account for the fact that cats, though they may kill them, won't eat them. It may also account for the otherwise inexplicable antipathy, and even fear, shown towards shrews in country lore.

Although they look like snakes, slow worms are actually legless lizards with movable eyelids, (unlike a snake). They are about 18 inches in length, and can be grey, black or dark brown, and if you are lucky enough to see one in the garden, by all means invite it to stay and it will repay you by feasting on slugs, snails and caterpillars. Like many other garden friends, it also tucks earthworms away with relish, but fortunately their reproductive rate is so good that earthworms easily outpace their many predators. Like hedgehogs, slow worms will also hibernate at the bottom of a bonfire heap, or something similar, so once again it would be kind not to disturb such piles in the winter if you can possibly avoid it.

Love them or hate them — and I hope it's the former — frogs and toads are also among your best friends in the garden. They both feed liberally on slugs, snails, caterpillars, woodlice and other insects, so if you have in your garden a pond, or a nice boggy patch of the kind that would make Eeyore feel at home, the chances are you'll win their co-operation. In the case of a pond, they will have no trouble getting in, but getting out will be a problem if it has sheer sides. If so, please remember to provide them with a ramp or a ladder and, in a hard winter, ensure that the pond doesn't freeze over. Whereas toads hibernate under flat stones, frogs burrow into the mud at the bottom of the pond, and need air.

The list of mammals, birds, insects and lizards that will help you wage war on slugs, snails and caterpillars is an impressive one and yet, despite their very best intentions, one thing is certain. A small army of the wretched creatures will survive to attack your flowers and vegetables because, like earthworms, their reproductive rate is phenomenal. So now it's your turn to roll up your sleeves and help the thrushes, toads, hedgehogs, slow worms and the rest who are striving on your behalf.

On the old estates, the under-gardeners used to do a daily round of the beds with a large jar of salt water into which they popped the slugs and snails they found. That's one tip, and that way you have only to dispose of the corpses. A mulch of oak leaves is an old recommendation for deterring them, but oak leaves aren't that easy to come by in a town centre. Gravel is a good modern equivalent, much in fashion, and bark chippings (the large, rough kind, not the smaller, smoother ones) are also a deterrent. But they are a deterrent only in the sense that they make the slug pause for thought while he works out his strategy for getting to the other side.

Another tip, much vaunted, is a saucer of beer sunk in the flower or vegetable bed, on the grounds that slugs cannot resist bitter (and it must be bitter, not lager, which slugs won't touch - they're too well brought up). They won't drink themselves to death, they will merely congregate, like wild animals round a water hole, so you must still gather up the inebriated bodies and dispose of them.

If that doesn't appeal to you, you can take a good handful of cabbage leaves and warm them gently in the oven without drying them out. Next, spread the leaves with dripping and lay them among the flowers and vegetables, and the following day you will have a splendid collection of slugs and snails to dispose of. The effects of a main meal of cabbage and dripping with a side bowl of beer are too awful to contemplate. It must all depend on your level of hysteria when contemplating the snail family in any other setting than a French restaurant.

And so we come to the animals that can be avoided no longer – moles. Are they friends or are they enemies? On the credit side, they are not after your plants, they're after earthworms and grubs. On the debit side, worms are friends and, if moles bestow the pleasure of their company on you, they throw up mounds of earth right across the lawn. It is at this point that you have to ask yourself if you are a pessimist or an optimist. If you look on the brighter side of life, you will tell yourself that you have just acquired a water drain which will help to keep the lawn in good shape, as well as some heaps of fine soil, full of beautifully mixed nutrients, which can be used in seed drills or, if you are brave enough to grow mushrooms, for covering the spawn. What the mole is doing is creating a small underground run, into which worms will drop or burrow, but every few feet he has to push the excavated earth to the surface. He will be content to use the same run unless flood or damage forces him to make a new one, or until the supply of worms is exhausted. In short, it's not as damaging as you think, and you can probably afford to live and let live.

If, on the other hand, you're of a more pessimistic turn of mind, you need to realise that mankind has been waging war on moles for centuries with striking lack of success. The mole catcher was a stalwart of country life until the 20th century was well advanced, charging a fee for the moles he caught which he then skinned, selling the skins on to the clothing industry for moleskin coats and wraps. Advice on how to get rid of moles has been handed down through the generations. At the end of the 16th century, Gerard confidently announced that garlic placed in a mole's run would do the trick, and that *"you shall see him run out, astonied."* The mole didn't, and it was Gerard who retired, astonished. Other wheezes for ridding yourself of moles include:

- pushing old fashioned camphor mothballs or Jeyes fluid down into the runs – and they must go right down into the runs themselves;

- planting *euphorbia lathyrus* or *euphorbia lactea* in the garden, since moles detest the smell – which is all very well but you can hardly have a garden and lawn consisting of nothing but euphorbia;

- smoking them out with so-called mole bombs, widely available, which must also be pushed well into the run;

- pushing the stick of a child's handheld windmill into the run, on the grounds that this will vibrate in the wind, and moles hate vibration;

- sinking empty bottles into the runs with their necks above ground so that the breeze blowing over the necks creates a booming effect in the run, also said to scare moles;

- you could also hang around for a day or two to see if you can catch the mole in the act of throwing up a new hill, creep softly up behind the quaking mound, push a spade deeply down behind it, lever it up and see if you've caught a mole. If you have, what are you going to do with it? Leap into your car and release it several miles away?

You will always find somebody to swear that one or other of these methods has worked, but a great many more to insist that they have not. If you do have a visitation, your best course of action may well be to count to a hundred and tell yourself that they're really sweet little creatures once you get to know them.

Finally, there are the wild animals in which the countryside is rich but, with the exception of the urban fox, are rarely seen where human habitations are to be found in any number – deer, badgers and foxes. Deer feature little in country lore and sayings, probably because they were a forbidden target for any hunter other than royalty and the nobility. Before the Norman Conquest, the forests had been open to all. After it, most became reserves closed for the hunting of boar and deer. The only activities in the forest normally permitted to ordinary folk were the gathering of firewood, and the autumn release of pigs to feed on acorns and beech mast, since these did not interfere with the life of red and roe deer which are our two native species.

It's now possible to encounter six types of deer in Britain. The Normans brought fallow deer over to join the red and the roe as hunting quarry. Sika, muntjac and chinese water deer are all 19th century arrivals, brought over to enhance their private parks by wealthy landowners who underestimated the ingenuity of their charges when it came to wriggling out of tight corners. The muntjac is the smallest, no larger than a medium-sized dog, and is distinguished from the chinese water deer only by a matter of a few inches and the fact that the latter has no antlers or horns. Roe deer, not much more than 2 feet (70cm) high at the shoulder, are

common throughout Britain. Living in small family groups, they are intensely shy, but have a great liking for roses and, in areas where they are not hunted, can sometimes be spotted in daytime. Fallow deer are larger, 3 feet (100 cm) or more at the shoulder, and although only occasionally found in Scotland and northern England, are common almost everywhere else. The mighty red deer, 4 feet high at the shoulder, is Britain's largest animal, and found mainly in mountains and on moorland in Scotland, northern and western England, and parts of East Anglia.

Red deer and roe deer are browsers, living on the leaves of trees and shrubs, whereas fallow deer mainly graze on grass and wild flowers and this is where, in a sense, the trouble starts. The amount of nutrition in leaves is limited, so huge quantities need to be consumed. If deer numbers rise too fast (the natural predators, bears and wolves, having long since disappeared from Britain) the supply of food comes under strain with unfortunate effects on the deer herds themselves, which become weakened, and on the regeneration and spread of woodland. There are also increasing complaints of deer being found stripping gardens on the edge of villages and towns and, in many wooded areas, the number of deer on the roads at night is rising.

If you are driving on roads with deer warning signs, it's well worth keeping at 40 m.p.h. or less. If a deer comes over a hedge in front of you – and they often do – the amount of damage you will do to each other has to be seen to be believed. If you and a deer are unlucky enough to be caught in this situation, ring the police and ask for their nearest wildlife officer (most rural areas have one or two). Whatever you do, don't try to help a wounded deer, however much you may want to. It is badly hurt, very frightened, and even a little muntjac can use its backward sloping horns in ways you'd rather not imagine!

Like most deer, badgers are nocturnal creatures, and you will rarely see a live one. Regrettably, you may well see dead ones on the road around August and, to a lesser extent, the turn of the year. Badger cubs are born around February, come out of the sett to play and learn from May onwards, and the young males leave to find and establish their own territories towards the end of the summer – hence the casualties in August as they begin to spread out into unfamiliar areas. The mature males – the expectant fathers - are driven away from the sett around the end of the year as the females prepare to give birth to a new litter. Knowing the territory better, they are less prone to death on the roads – but not immune.

At first sight, the entrance to a badger sett could be mistaken for that of a large rabbit hole. The tell tale signs are that there will be at least two entrances (often many more – badgers are such expert diggers that one sometimes feels they dig for the sheer pleasure of it), and that the main entrance will show signs of regular use with little piles of discarded bedding, made of bracken, leaves or grass, nearby. Badgers are remarkably clean and tidy and change their bedding with the fastidious frequency of a five star hotel. The first appearance of a badger from its sett as night falls may well be that of a large posterior as its owner emerges backwards, dragging out the old bedding tucked under its chin. What other animal would enter the world bottom first? It is a sign that the badger has no enemies (man, as ever, apart). Badgers live principally on earthworms, which their remarkable powers of smell can detect several inches deep, but they will also eat snails, mice, wasps, blackberries, fallen apples and the like. The chances of a badger turning up in your garden are very small – but it can happen, and in such event its immensely strong claws can trash a garden with remarkable speed. Although they are not aggressive, they can be determined if they scent food, so phone the police wildlife officer or your local badger protection group for assistance.

Badgers are omnivorous, but cautious, animals and, being nocturnal, hardly figure in the folklore of the countryside apart from the unsubstantiated calumny that they carry cattle tuberculosis. Foxes, on the other hand, have an ages-old reputation for slyness and cunning from the ways in which they twist and turn to escape trouble when hunted. A fox will double back on itself, take to water, climb trees and even mingle with a flock of sheep to disguise its strong scent and throw its pursuers off course.

Like badgers, foxes are omnivorous, but with even wider tastes, which include birds, chickens and their eggs — one reason they top the most-wanted list of farmers and smallholders (if you come across a pile of bird-feathers in a field and the feathers have been cleanly bitten off you will know it is a fox that did the damage — a bird of prey tears them out). At the same time, foxes are lazy hunters. They will cross a couple of fields or the local park to rootle for scraps in your dustbin rather than chase a rabbit in the same hedgerow if it is less bother. This is a pity, because when rabbit numbers get out of control the habitats around them are degraded, to the detriment of other wildlife and, ultimately, the rabbits themselves. In this, as in the whole natural world, the right balance between species is essential for the health of each. If one grows out of control it damages the rest, to which the exploding population of homo sapiens bears witness across the world.